D1179806

Oral Roberts

Oral Roberts

the
4TH
man

AND OTHER FAMOUS SERMONS

*Exactly as Oral Roberts
preached them from
the Revival Platform.*

HEALING WATERS, INC. *Tulsa, Oklahoma*
1951

Contents

THE FOURTH MAN

one | **The Fourth Man**

Like a glittering diamond on a couch of velvet, the city of Jerusalem is set among the hills of Judea, in the exact geographical center of the earth. It is the city of God the King. In Jerusalem the temple of Jehovah stood in its magnificent glory, upon its altars were offered sacrifices, blood was shed for the forgiveness of the people of God. Prophets walked the streets of Jerusalem proclaiming the way of the Lord; Priests chanted their rituals and the law of God went forth in the land.

God placed His name in Jerusalem and met with His people there.

Far away from Jerusalem was another city: the greatest city the pride and skill of man ever built. Its walls were three hundred feet high and wide enough at the top for eight chariots to run races side by side. Inside the walls of Babylon was the palace of Nebuchadnezzar which was more like a fortress for it was surrounded by walls seven miles around. Nearby were the famous "hanging gardens," that Nebuchadnezzar built for his wife and that became one of the wonders of the ancient world. The beautiful river Euphrates wound its way through Babylon adding much to the wondrous beauty of the city.

3

The heathen temple Bel was situated in the very heart of the city, its spires towered six hundred feet skyward. On its altars were offered animals which had been strangled to death and which later were sold in the meat shops of Babylon. This is why young Daniel and his companions declared: "We will not defile ourselves with the king's meat." They refused to eat meat from animals which had been sacrificed to idol gods.

Nebuchadnezzar was the proudest king that ever sat on an earthly throne. His armies had conquered the world and at the time the three Hebrew children were captured and brought to Babylon he was the undisputed ruler of the world.

One day Nebuchadnezzar led his crack legions across the burning, shimmering sands of the desert and laid siege to Jerusalem where the people of God had turned away from the paths of righteousness and were violating His sacred laws.

With their battering rams the Babylonians tore down the walls of the "city of the great king," plundered and sacked Jerusalem, destroyed the temple and as trophies of their victory led captive the very flower of the nation. Among the captives were the three Hebrew children: Shadrach, Meshach and Abednego.

Standing on one of the hills overlooking their ruined city, these young Hebrew princes said in their melancholy, "O Jerusalem, O Jerusalem, if we forget thee let our right hand forget its cunning and our tongue cleave to the roof of our mouth."

Weeks later they passed inside the gates of Babylon, captives to a heathen king. They were led down to the banks of the Euphrates where the curious Babylonians came to gaze on them. "Play for us on your instruments," said the Babylonians, "sing for us some of the songs of Zion." They replied, "How can we sing the songs of our God in a strange land?"

Scarcely had they become accustomed to the splendor of their surroundings until they heard the sound of all kinds of music and everywhere about them the Babylonians fell prostrate to the ground, clasping their hands together and crying,

"Great is Nebuchadnezzar our God!
There is no God in the earth but Nebuchadnezzar!"

Shadrach, Meshach, and Abednego were astounded. The Babylonians were worshiping Nebuchadnezzar, a man, as God. They stood their ground refusing to bow. "Thou shalt have no other Gods before me," their God had commanded. The Lord Jehovah was the only true God, whether in Babylon or Jerusalem, or in heaven or earth.

RELIGION WILL BE TRIED

These three young men came face to face with an inescapable fact: true religion will be tried. Whether these boys live in Jerusalem or Babylon they will be tried. The devil will be after them.

A Methodist Bishop was traveling across the United States on a preaching mission. His train pulled into a little town for a brief stop. He saw the colored porter standing nearby. "Porter!" the Bishop called.

"Whatcha want, boss?"

"I would like to ask you about the religious condition of the people in your town. Is there anyone here who has old-time religion?"

"Yes suh, plenty of folks 'round heah have religion."

"Is the devil after any of them?" the Bishop asked.

The porter smiled and quick as a flash replied, "Yes suh, the devil is after them that's *got it*."

The devil *is* after the people who have old-time religion. I know. He is after me.

It matters not where you live or where you travel, your religious convictions will be tried. Thousands of people are severely tried even while attending our campaigns.

One night a beautiful young girl responded to my call to the unsaved. She was gloriously saved. She returned to her chair with shining eyes and a burning heart. She said to her boy friend, "O it's wonderful what Jesus has done for me tonight. Come on and go with me to the prayer tent. I want you to receive Jesus as your Saviour too."

He laughed in her face.

She didn't know what to do or say. When he continued to laugh and poke fun at her she turned to him, looked him full in the face and said very quietly, "All right, if you won't go to heaven with me, I am not going to hell with you!"

This young woman was made out of the right kind of stuff. She knew where she was going. She wanted others to go with her. But one thing sure: *she* was going, even if she had to go alone.

A few months ago I received a beseeching letter from a woman whose husband was up-and-down and in-and-out in his religious experience. It seemed that he had been re-claimed in one of our meetings and for a few months there-after, he was very religious. But now he was beginning to backslide again.

She wanted to know if I would let him join my party and travel with me all the time. "I just know he'll stay saved if he could be around you all the time," she wrote.

I thought about it for a moment. Then I realized that religion is not a thing of environment, it is an attitude of the heart. It is inner peace and power brought into the spirit by the power of God when a person repents of his sins and gets right with his God. If one will cultivate the spirit of Christ in his heart it will give him vast strength, great principles to live by, and an ever-increasing faith.

But religion gives power to a man's life only when he *wants* to serve God as a matter of principle, when he makes it his attitude and desire. Although he might receive very definite help from another Christian yet his own religion is sufficient to enable him to live victoriously and courageously in any circumstance, condition or environment. Isn't that right? If you believe that, say, "Amen."

So I reasoned that if the woman's husband lived where he could attend church and practice his faith in God that he should have no difficulty keeping his religion for his religion would keep him. A man just has to practice his faith, that's all. What good would it do to let him join my party. We are on the front lines in this battle for God. It is dangerous up here where the devil is contesting every step I take and fighting me from all sides. What would this man do up here where the battle is really hot if he can't stay saved even in the quiet and safety of his own home?

No, the only answer to his problem is to dig down to the bedrock of real heart-felt religion and anchor his soul forever on the Rock of Ages. When he really wants God's way and daily practices his faith in God he will find that circumstances and environment will have absolutely no power over him; his faith will open up a path for him in the wilderness, create an oasis for him in the desert, and will make him feel like "running through a troop and jumping over a wall."

Shadrach, Meshach and Abednego refused to bow and

were reported to Nebuchadnezzar. The informers said, "O king, there are three young men in your kingdom who refuse to bow to your image!"

Enraged, he cried, "Bring them to me."

Shortly, Shadrach, Meshach and Abednego stood before the king. "Is it true, that when you hear the sound of music, you do not fall down and worship me?"

They nodded.

"Perhaps, you don't understand then," he said.

They understood.

"Now I will give you another chance," Nebuchadnezzar said. "If and when you hear the sound of any kind of music, you fall down and worship me, well and good."

He saw them stiffen.

He said, "I warn you. Whether you realize it or not *I* am god. Why, I have captured not only the nations of the earth, I have captured all their gods as well. I have a stockpile of gods here in Babylon. I have become god myself."

Shadrach, Meshach and Abednego set their shoulders, they knew what was coming.

Nebuchadnezzar continued, "When I captured Jerusalem, I couldn't find your God. He seems to have no physical likeness or earthly form. Therefore, you have no God. Now, if you don't bow down and worship my image I will cast you alive into the midst of a burning fiery furnace and who will be that God that shall deliver you out of my hands?"

GOD IS ABLE

Without a moment's hesitation, without the flicker of an eyelash, they said, "Our God whom we serve is able to deliver us!"

He is able!

Thank God, our God *is able!*

Let the angels shout it, "Our God is able!"

Let weakness lie limp on His shoulder, "Our God is able!"

Bring forth the royal diadem, "Our God is able!"

Let the heathen rage and imagine a vain thing, "Our God is able!"

Let the hosts of hell assail, "Our God is able!"

Let the devil roar in his fury, "Our God is able!"

Let the kings of the earth tremble, "Our God is able!"

Let Nebuchadnezzar heat his furnace seven times hotter than ordinary, "Our God is able!"

Shadrach, Meshach and Abednego knew God was able. They were not saying He was able in order to bolster their own courage, they were speaking out of knowledge and experience. The record of their God was that He *is* able. The prophets declared it. The Psalmist sang it. The children of Israel danced on the sands of the Red Sea and shouted that He was able. They remembered His outstretched hand, they had knowledge of His spirit. They believed this so strongly that they felt that their God—unseen and invisible—was more real to them than the impostor standing before them in his blasphemous assumption.

"Our God whom we serve is able," they shouted. (God is always able to those who *serve* Him.) "Our God is able to deliver us," they said, "and He will deliver us out of thy hand, O king."

They knew God was able.

They knew God would deliver them.

They knew that they would be delivered from the king's hands.

Such was the power of their faith in God.

Nebuchadnezzar had succeeded in locking them within the walls of Babylon but he could not lock their God *out*.

He had isolated them from their environment but he could not separate them from their God. He had carted them away from the city of the great King but he could not keep the great King from going with them.

God was with Shadrach, Meshach and Abednego and they knew it. His presence was real enough for them to refuse to bow. They knew in their refusal God would deliver them.

This is a wonderful thing to know. Everyone who knows God can know it. But He must be your God and you must serve Him.

The three Hebrew children did not stop by declaring their God whom they served was able to deliver them and would deliver them. They said, "But if not, we will not bow down to thy image or serve thy gods."

This was the first time anyone ever had the courage and faith to tell the old blasphemous king to get in his place. He was enraged and became panic-stricken. He recognized the seeds of rebellion and knew that if they were not destroyed his kingdom could not last. Screaming for his most powerful soldiers, he commanded them to heat the furnace and throw Shadrach, Meshach and Abednego in it to burn so he could make them a lesson to the people in his kingdom.

"And Nebuchadnezzar commanded the most mighty men in his army to bind Shadrach, Meshach and Abednego." (He had a healthy respect for the servants of God.)

These men bound Shadrach, Meshach and Abednego with their clothes on. The king's commandment was urgent and the fire hot.

In their haste to cast them into the furnace the soldiers got a little too close to the fire themselves and were *consumed*. They weren't made out of the right kind of stuff.

FATE OF A COMPROMISER

Who were these soldiers? They were closest to the king, his most trusted men. They polished his boots and bowed before him and did his bidding. What did they get out of it? When they got close enough to the fire to feel it they were fragile and combustible. They could not endure.

Compromisers pay an awful price.

Shadrach, Meshach and Abednego said, "We may burn but we won't bow." They were perfectly willing to suffer for their religion but they would not compromise.

But they found out when they would not bow they *could not burn!*

When the soldiers who bowed came near the fire they burned! Compromisers will burn!

One of the best men I ever knew found this out. He fell in love with my ministry of Bible deliverance. "Brother Roberts, this is wonderful," he said to me, "I never knew God was so good before!" He was healed through my prayers and got a very definite lift for his own ministry. He began preaching with new zeal and power. He was stirring people for he had a revival kindling in his soul.

One day a prominent member of his church called him off to one side and told him that if he didn't stop preaching the way he was the church would kick him out. My friend cooled off and in a few days he became exceedingly cool to me. I heard of certain statements he made against my ministry in order to justify his compromise. His true friends were crushed but when they would talk to him they had no effect at all. In two months he dried up in his soul, became very bitter and soon was actively opposed to God's ministry of deliverance.

I fell on my knees and prayed to God to save him from his folly for I know the fate of men who compromise their convictions. But my prayers were not enough. He had made his decision to bow and therefore he must burn.

Months passed. One day someone came to me in tears and said, "Brother Roberts, have you heard about Brother so-and-so?"

I said, "No, what has happened?"

"His church has kicked him out without mercy."

"I am not surprised. How is he taking it?"

"He is crushed. He sees his mistake. He says he never should have compromised."

And neighbor, that is right; he never should have compromised.

You will always lose the thing you gained by compromise. If you *bow* you will *burn*. But if you will not bow, you cannot burn. God will take care of you.

The outcome of my friend's experience is that once more he has opened his heart to preach God's power to set men free in soul, mind and body. He has seen his mistake. He now realizes that you win only by obeying God, not man. He said to me, "Brother Roberts, had I known then what I know now perhaps I could have saved my church and myself. As it is I am practically starting over. I've got to take up where I left off."

THINGS WE HAVE COMPROMISED

Many people in the church are compromising their testimony. Old convictions once dear to the heart of the church are being stifled and in their place there is compromise. Many outstanding ministers who once preached under the anointing of the Holy Ghost have bowed to certain groups in their midst and today they are *burning*.

I smell the scorching of human souls, the smell of fire is on our garments.

I charge the church with three grievous compromises:

Bible Holiness. Heart purity, clean living, separation from the world, holiness of life. The word "holiness" has become an abomination unto us. We have turned up our nose to holiness. We are ashamed to use that word in our preaching and our conversation. But God loves holiness. "Holiness unto the Lord," is one of the famous slogans of the Bible. The Hebrew writer urged the people to holiness for he said ". . . without holiness no man shall see the Lord."

The experience of sanctification which produces holiness of heart and life has become a byword, something to be looked down on by the ecclesiastical groups. But God says, "This is the will of God even your sanctification."

I think I see signs of a turning back to holiness, even among some of the churches who have been so hostile to it. They are beginning to realize that to have power you must first be holy and set apart from the world.

The only successful way to handle the problem of worldliness in the church is to preach Bible holiness until our people have become holy. No man can be separated from the world until first he is separated unto God. Holiness of heart is a pure love for God and a holy hatred of sin. Holiness is the dividing line. It is the great separator of the spirit from the flesh, heaven from hell, righteousness and sin.

Worldliness is selfishness, it is living as one pleases, doing as the world does. Worldliness is an attitude that permeates the whole life. We look on a person who is living a worldly life and say, "He is worldly." We have observed his bad habits, his intemperance and by those acts declare him to be worldly. He is manifesting what he is within. There is no use to preach to him that he should quit his bad habits, we must show him the way of holiness, directing him to consecrate his life to God so that he can be sanctified holy. God will then take out of his heart the very appetite and desire for worldly things. Holiness cures from within. It is the glorious liberation of the whole life from any impurity and from all worldly desires. And it is the redirecting of the life in those channels of unselfish service to mankind. In a word, holiness is unselfishness. But no man can be holy until first he consecrates himself and is sanctified by the blood of Christ.

We must make room in our doctrines, our preaching, our church emphasis and our daily lives for bible holiness—unselfishness of heart and life.

The Baptism of the Holy Ghost. I charge the church with compromising the powerful experience of the Upper Room, the Holy Ghost and fire which the disciples received on Pentecost morning. No one knows the importance of the Holy Ghost like God does. He *commanded* the disciples to "Tarry until" they were "endued with power from on high," for he said, "ye shall be baptized with the Holy Ghost not many days hence."

The baptism of the Holy Ghost then was a definite thing to be received, the disciples were commanded to tarry before the Lord until they received it. They were promised it in a few days; they actually received it ten days later *and* when they received it *things began to happen.*

It is important that they spoke with tongues as the Spirit gave utterance but more important that in receiving the Holy Ghost as a personal enduement of power from on high they were "fired up" and "empowered" to go forth to the people, preaching the risen Jesus whom the people had just crucified. It took a lot of courage and power to face the howling mobs that crucified their Saviour. But the Holy Ghost supplied that power.

The baptism of the Holy Ghost did many things to the disciples, three of them stand out above the others: this experience gave them power to win souls, it gave them power to heal the sick, it gave them power to stand persecution. In all these things they, "walked in the comfort of the Holy Ghost."

I'll tell you why we are not winning very many lost souls, why we are failing to heal the sick, why we have little persecution: we have compromised our attitude and belief toward the baptism of the Holy Ghost.

God cannot bless us in our compromising. The smell of fire is on our garments. And the thing that hurts most of all is that *if we would change our attitude and actually tarry before our God and receive the same Holy Ghost experience as they did at Pentecost we could and would win tens of thousands more souls, bring healing to multitudes and would count it the rarest honor to suffer shame for Jesus' sake!*

If you believe that, say, "Amen!"

Healing. We have compromised on our Lord's sweet compassion to heal and his willingness to deliver our sick and afflicted.

I said to one of the leading preachers of this generation, a man who is winning many souls but who has no heart of compassion toward the sick and afflicted, a man who feels no burden to carry out our Lord's command to "heal the sick and cast out devils"—to him I said, "My brother, what are you going to do about the healing of the sick?"

He replied, "I am leaving them to you."

I said, "Thank you, I gladly accept them."

Our Saviour came into this world of sin and sickness and demon-power saying, "The spirit of the Lord is upon me, because he hath anointed me to preach the gospel to the poor; he hath sent me to heal the brokenhearted, to preach deliverance to the captives, and recovering of sight to the blind, to set at liberty them that are bruised."

This same Jesus later said, "The thief cometh not but for to steal and to kill; I am come that they might have life and that they might have it more abundantly."

Peter described Jesus' ministry by one comprehensive statement: "God anointed Jesus of Nazareth with the Holy Ghost and power, who went about doing good, healing all who were oppressed of the devil, for God was with him."

Jesus charged his disciples to "heal the sick and to cast out devils." He never sent forth a disciple to preach without charging him to heal the people's sicknesses. Many of the disciples returned to Jesus with great joy, saying, "Lord, even the devils are subject unto us through thy name."

Yet today an alarming number of ministers and churches have closed their hearts to the suffering of human life. They have no healing ministry, they make no effort to show the almighty power of faith over sickness and demon-power. "Thy faith doth make thee whole," is seldom said to those who would be healed through faith if they only had guidance and inspiration.

The prophet Jeremiah describes these churches and ministers: "You have healed the hurt of my people only slightly."

What an indictment against the church that carries the name of Jesus. And yet everyone of us knows beyond the shadow of a doubt that if Jesus were here among us today in the flesh that he would still heal the sick and cast out devils. The roads would be lined with thousands bringing their sick to Jesus for healing. Not a one of them would be turned away.

Men and women, what is wrong with us today? Why have we allowed ourselves to backslide from our healing faith? Why are we paying preachers their weekly salaries to hear them tell us, "The days of miracles are over," when down deep inside us we know that "Jesus Christ is the same yesterday, today and forever!" Why? Why?

We must arouse ourselves. Jesus is coming soon. We must work quickly to snatch men from hell and to heal the sick in our midst. This is no time to fuss and fume, to bicker and quarrel, to split theological hairs over points of doctrine—this is the time to carry out our Lord's command to *deliver* our generation.

LIFE'S FIERY FURNACES

Shadrach, Meshach and Abednego said, "We may burn but we won't bow." The angry king finally succeeded in having them thrown with all their clothes on into the burning fiery furnace. They slammed the door shut and stood back, waiting for the fire to consume the three Hebrew children.

Life's fiery furnaces. How real they are today. Hundreds of people in this great audience of over 8,000 people have been thrown into fiery furnaces heated seven times hot. You have been thrust into the furnace for your testimony, your integrity and conviction. You wouldn't bow.

Some of you have had some of your dearest friendships betrayed.

I know how hot that furnace is for I too have had many of my friendships betrayed. Some of my friends have given no reason; they simply have turned their backs. I know of no furnace hotter than the loss of friendship.

Sometimes the fiery furnace that opens its burning mouth to sear us is financial setback and material loss.

Lee Braxton, our National radio director, faced this furnace over twenty years ago. At that time he was earning only $30.00 a week as an automobile mechanic. One day he repaired a man's car so well that the man offered him a job at $70.00 a week if he would manage his garage for him. Lee gladly accepted. Then the man told him that he would have to work on Sunday. That was against Lee's religion. He had been taught to keep the Lord's day holy. He saw the extra $40.00 a week, which his family needed, slip between his fingers.

A few months ago when he was telling me about this, I asked him what he said to the man. He said, "I'm sorry, sir, but I can't take the job. It would violate my convictions about the Sabbath day."

"Then what did you do?" I asked.

"I went back to my job making $30.00 a week. In a few short weeks an opportunity for advancement far greater than the $70.00 a week came to me. Not only would this new opportunity increase my wages far beyond what I had been offered but I did not have to work on Sunday."

I said, "Lee, if you had it to do over what would you do?"

"I would do exactly as I did. I would put God first. He has blessed me a thousand times above my expectations."

Sometimes life's fiery furnaces burn fiercely with sickness and affliction. We have been well and strong all our lives and suddenly we are laid low with a terrible affliction. I know, I have had tuberculosis in both lungs. What a hot furnace this is.

Job was smitten with sore boils from head to toe, was deserted by his wife, was ridiculed and accused by men who claimed to be his friends, was left alone on an ash heap outside an oriental village. But he wouldn't bow. When his wife said, "Curse God and die," he replied, "You speak as a foolish woman." When his friends declared God had forsaken him, he cried, "I know my redeemer liveth." Job held true and soon was gloriously healed.

Shadrach, Meshach and Abednego were cast into the midst of the furnace in Babylon. A few minutes passed. The furnace rumbled on its foundations and white-hot flames leaped skyward. The three Hebrew children were in those flames.

Pretty soon Nebuchadnezzar came near the mouth of the furnace and looked in. When he did he was astonished. He shouted to his princes and governors, "Come here, quick!"

"Did not we cast three men bound into the fire?" he shouted.

"True, O king," his men replied.

"Look!" he cried. "Look! I see four men loose and they are walking in the midst of the flames! And the form of the fourth is like unto the Son of God!"

Hallelujah!

The Fourth Man had come to help Shadrach, Meshach and Abednego in the urgency of their need. He had subdued the crackling flames, robbed the fire of its sting, torn off the bonds of his servants, lifted them up and while the old king watched he was walking arm-in-arm with the three Hebrew children right in the middle of the flames.

Let me recapitulate: When Shadrach, Meshach and Abednego hung their harps on the willows, refusing to sing the songs of Zion to the mocking Babylonians, a thrill went through heaven. When the music sounded and Babylonians fell to the ground chanting praises to Nebuchadnezzar, the three Hebrew children stood erect. All heaven was alerted.

When they stood before the king and declared they might burn but they wouldn't bow, the Son of God said, "If you won't bow, I'll see to it that you won't burn!"

When the soldiers threw these boys into the furnace, the Fourth Man hurled himself through space and in a moment's time was at their side going into the burning fiery furnace with them. By the time the door was shut he had ripped off their bonds, and clothed them with divine asbestos. When the king looked in, all four of them were walking around in the fire, unhurt and untouched by the flames. The form of the Fourth Man was like the Son of God.

Who is this Fourth Man?
In Genesis he is the Seed of the Woman,
In Exodus he is the Passover Lamb,
In Leviticus he is Our High Priest,
In Numbers he is the Pillar of Cloud by day and the Pillar of Fire by night,
In Deuteronomy he is the Prophet like unto Moses,
In Joshua he is the Captain of our Salvation,
In Judges he is our Judge and Lawgiver,
In Ruth he is our Kinsman Redeemer,
In I and II Samuel he is our Trusted Prophet,
In Kings and Chronicles he is our Reigning King,
In Ezra he is the Rebuilder of the Broken Down Walls of Human Life,
In Esther he is our Mordecai,
and in Job he is our Ever-Living Redeemer,
   "For I know my redeemer liveth."
Who is this Fourth Man?
In Psalms he is our Shepherd,
In Proverbs and Ecclesiastes he is our Wisdom,
In the Song of Solomon he is our Lover and Bridegroom,
In Isaiah he is the Prince of Peace,
In Jeremiah he is the Righteous Branch,
In Lamentations he is our Weeping Prophet,

In Ezekial he is the wonderful Four-Faced Man,
and in Daniel the Fourth Man in "Life's Fiery Furnaces."

Who is this Fourth Man?

In Hosea he is the Faithful Husband,
   "Forever married to the backslider,"
In Joel he is the Baptizer with the Holy Ghost and Fire,
In Amos he is our Burden-Bearer,
In Obadiah he is the Mighty to Save,
In Jonah he is our great Foreign Missionary,
In Micah he is the Messenger of Beautiful Feet,
In Nahum he is the Avenger of God's Elect,
In Habakkuk he is God's Evangelist, crying,
   "Revive thy work in the midst of the years,"
In Zephaniah he is our Saviour,
In Haggai he is the Restorer of God's Lost Heritage,
In Zechariah he is the Fountain opened up in the House
   of David for Sin and Uncleanness,
In Malachi he is the Sun of Righteousness, rising with
   Healing in His Wings.

Who is this Fourth Man?

In Matthew he is the Messiah,
In Mark he is the Wonder-Worker,
In Luke he is the Son of Man,
In John he is the Son of God,
In Acts he is the Holy Ghost,
In Romans he is our Justifier,
In I and II Corinthians he is our Sanctifier,
In Galatians he is our Redeemer from the Curse of the
   Law,
In Ephesians he is the Christ of Unsearchable Riches,
In Philippians he is the God Who Supplies all our
   Needs,

In Colossians he is the Fulness of the Godhead Bodily,
In I and II Thessalonians he is our Soon Coming King,
In I and II Timothy he is our Mediator between God and Man,
In Titus he is our Faithful Pastor,
In Philemon he is a Friend that Sticketh Closer than a Brother.
Who is this Fourth Man?
In Hebrews he is the Blood of the Everlasting Covenant,
In James he is our Great Physician, for
  "The prayer of faith shall save the sick,"
In I and II Peter he is our Chief Shepherd
  Who soon shall appear with a Crown of Unfading Glory,
In I, II and III John he is Love,
In Jude he is the Lord coming with Ten Thousands of His Saints,
And in Revelation he is the King of Kings and Lord of Lords!

WHO IS THIS FOURTH MAN?

He is Abel's Sacrifice, Noah's Rainbow, Abraham's Ram, Isaac's Wells, Jacob's Ladder, Issachar's Burdens, Jacob's Sceptre, Balaam's Shiloh, Moses' Rod, Joshua's Sun and Moon that stood still, Elijah's Mantle, Elisha's Staff, Gideon's Fleece, Samuel's Horn of Oil, David's Slingshot, Isaiah's Fig Poultice, Hezekiah's Sundial, Daniel's Visions, Amos' Burden and Malachi's Sun of Righteousness.

Who is this Fourth Man?

He is Peter's Shadow, Stephen's Signs and Wonders, Paul's Handkerchiefs and Aprons and John's Pearly White City.

Who is this Fourth Man?

He is a Father to the Orphan, Husband to the Widow, to the traveler in the night he is the Bright and Morning Star, to those who walk in the Lonesome Valley he is the Lily of the Valley, the Rose of Sharon and Honey in the Rock.

He is the Brightness of God's Glory, the Express Image of His Person, the King of Glory, the Pearl of Great Price, the Rock in a Weary Land, the Cup that runneth over, the Rod and Staff that comfort and the Government of our life is upon his shoulders.

Who is this Fourth Man?

He is Jesus of Nazareth, the Son of the living God! My Saviour, my companion, my Lord and King!

UNTOUCHED BY THE FIRE

The Fourth Man was not responsible for Nebuchadnezzar's infamous act of throwing Shadrach, Meshach and Abednego into the burning fiery furnace but he became responsible for bringing them out, he did not stoke the furnace but he did rob the fire of its violence, he did not bind them but he did liberate them from their bonds, he did not send them into the furnace but he did bring them out.

Another thing I want you to see tonight is that the three Hebrew children were freer and had more liberty *inside* the furnace than they did before they were thrown in. Before they were cast into the furnace they were bound, once they were inside, their bonds were ripped off. They were thrown down bound into the midst of the fire, now they are loose and walking around in the furnace heated seven-times hot.

THE KING IS CONVERTED

Nebuchadnezzar shouted, "Shadrach, Meshach and Abednego come forth and come hither."

They came forth, rejoicing and praising God. The king began to examine their clothes and bodies. He smelled of their hair, felt of their clothes, put his hands on their faces. "The smell of fire has not passed on their garments, neither is the hair of their head singed," he said solemnly.

Because of their love for God they would not bow; because of their faith God would not let them burn.

By this time the Fourth Man had vanished. He was on his way to deliver someone else who was even then saying, "I will not bow."

Nebuchadnezzar called for his scribes and commanded them to write:

"Then Nebuchadnezzar spake, and said, Blessed be the God of Shadrach, Meshach, and Abednego, who hath sent his angel, and delivered his servants that trusted in him, and have changed the king's word, and yielded their bodies that they might not serve nor worship any god, except their own God.

Therefore, I make a decree, That every people, nation, and language, which speak any thing amiss against the God of Shadrach, Meshach, and Abednego, shall be cut in pieces, and their houses shall be made a dunghill: because there is no other God that can deliver after this sort."

I can think of no better way to close this message on the Fourth Man than to repeat Nebuchadnezzar's great declaration of faith:

"There is no other God that can deliver after this sort."

Every head bowed please.

SAMSON AND DELILAH—
BATTLE OF CHAMPIONS

Scripture Text: Judges 16

two | Samson and Delilah—Battle of Champions

This is a story of love and romance; of lust and passion; of cunning and intrigue; of a woman's charms and a man's faith. It is a battle between two champions, each from a world against the other, each representing their own God, their own people, each fighting to the death. It is a romance between two young people, a boy and a girl who never should have loved, who never should have taken the first kiss, who never should have stirred each other's passions, who never should have lain in each other's arms.

In the background there were two mighty forces, on the one hand the devil who believes that in every person there is a weakness which if the person yields to him (the devil) that he can drag that person down to the lowest hell, and on the other hand God who believes that in every person there is a power, a strength, through which if that person yields to God, He can lift him to the highest heaven.

This story goes back to the birth of a little baby, a little tousle-headed boy, who was named Samson by the angels even before he was born. This child was born as a sign (for a purpose) that God would deliver His people. The Philistines had overrun the country of Judea. The people of God had been oppressed by them for many years and throughout

27

the length and breadth of the land you could hear the tramp, tramp, of marching feet of rough soldiers who had swords in their hands which they held over the heads of the people of God and by which they exacted heavy burdens and levied terrible taxes. The whole land was in the grip of bondage to Philistia and throughout the land oppressed people were praying and crying unto God, regretting their backsliding, their going away from God which resulted in their country being oppressed by the hand of the Philistine. God always moves when men pray, when people seek His face because of the oppression of the devil's power, when they humble themselves and pray and repent of their sins and confess their sins to God—God will hear their prayer, God will forgive their sins, God will heal their land. He heard the cry of His people and had a little baby born in the home of Mr. and Mrs. Manoah, a humble little family off to one side of Israel, in Dan.

One day Mrs. Manoah was approached by an angel of heaven. He said unto her, "God has heard the cry of His people and you shall conceive a son and shall call his name Samson, and this child shall be God's child. He will be a Nazarite unto God, never let him put wine to his lips, never cut his hair for his hair shall be a symbol of his consecration and in his consecration he shall be strong, and the spirit of God shall come upon his arms and no one's arms shall be as strong as Samson's." When Mr. Manoah came home, the angel came to him too, and together this man and his wife believed God. In due process of time little Samson was born; God remembered His people.

One day the soldiers of the Philistines marched through the land exacting their heavy taxes. They passed the home of the Manoahs. Little Samson lay asleep in his mother's arms. They little knew that one day that little baby there in his mother's arms would lift up his hands and slay a thousand of them before the sun went down. As they marched by that humble little home in Dan they did not know that someday that child would take the jawbone of a mule and win a tremendous battle over them. Walk softly, Philistines, that baby someday will wrench the gates of your city from their hinges, throw them across his shoulders and carry them to the top of the hill and set them down as trophy of his victory over the oppressors of the people of God. Philistines, if you knew this child's destiny, his faith as a man, you would shake in your boots. If you knew this young man will skip over the hills of Israel in his power, in his glory, in his faith and fearlessness you would cower in his presence. They little knew that—had they known, they would have spoken softly when they came to the home of Mr. and Mrs. Manoah.

I thank God tonight that whenever oppression comes, God stretches out His hand—a little baby is born here, a child is raised up over there, some boy feels the call of God, some girl hears God speak to her. All because humanity is being oppressed. Their cry is coming up to God, "Help us God! Come to our deliverance!" Many consecrated people are feeling a strange moving of the holy spirit. The signs of God are once more in evidence and again the power of God is marching across the earth to bring deliverance to lost and suffering humanity.

This child was given a sign—his hair was to grow long forming seven locks. The word "seven" means *completeness*. This was God's sign.

God has always moved by signs. In the New Testament we are told of three signs, or signs in a threefold manner. He said, "THESE SIGNS shall follow them that believe." In the book of Acts we are told of *"many signs"* which God performed through the early christians. In the book of Romans we are told of *"mighty signs"* which followed the ministry of the apostle Paul. "These signs," "many signs," "mighty signs" and *every* sign is the indication that God is moving again in human affairs.

The presence of God I feel in my *right hand* is a sign, another indication of the love of God for the oppressed. God places a high premium upon human deliverance and happiness. As long as there is one man unhappy and one woman unhappy and one child sick and afflicted, the signs of God's deliverance will be performed to set people free. Signs of deliverance—a man's hand or a man's heart or a man's message, some way God will deal with that person and he will become a deliverer. I tell you, neighbor, now is the time to have faith in God for deliverers are being raised up. Once again hope is coming to our people. We are getting a new faith, a new vision, a new revelation. We are living in an hour pregnant with destiny, when the power of God is coming down to deliver us, to set us free and to make us perfectly whole.

THE CHAMPION

When Samson was grown he was going through the woods one day when a young lion sprang out upon him. Not an old lion but a young lion. The spirit of God came upon Samson like a strong wind, going through every fiber of his being; his *ordinary* arms became the arms of steel and he reached out and took hold of the lion and rent his body in pieces as he would tear a lamb in his hands.

One day the Philistines trapped Samson in their city and at midnight when he rose to leave, he found the gates locked. Looking up to God he prayed. The spirit of God came upon him, once more his hands were like steel and he lifted the gates off their hinges and carried them to the top of the hill.

One day the Philistines said to the people of Israel, "Deliver unto our hands, Samson. If you don't we will oppress you even more."

So they came to Samson and said, "Samson, we must deliver you unto the hands of the Philistines."

He said, "You may bind me on one condition: promise me that you won't fall upon me yourselves."

So they promised him. They bound him hand and foot and delivered him to the army of Philistia. Binding him to a chariot they dragged him back to Philistia. But about sundown the spirit of God seized Samson's body and once more his hands became bands of steel. He rose up and threw the bonds off as though they were twine strings and seizing the jawbone of a dead mule he waded into that bunch of uncircumcised Philistines and when the sun went down beneath the western horizon they counted a thousand dead soldiers and Samson stood on the hill shouting the glory of God.

In every home in Israel Samson was discussed. The little children paraded like little champions. Samson's name was on every tongue and even the old, old men said, "Samson is our hope!" From one end of the land unto the other the cry went up, "Samson shall deliver us! Samson shall deliver us!" Oh what a wonderful thing it is for God to raise up deliverers to renew hope in the hearts of men.

God has men and God has women He has laid His hands upon in these days. I have never seen such hope in men's faces as I see across America today. I have never dealt with preachers who have such faith as I am dealing with tonight! A new spirit is among us and it is a wonderful thing that God has Samsons—champions—on the march again.

PLAYING WITH GOD'S SIGN

Samson had one weakness. He played with God's signs. He teased his lover with God's sign. Through God's sign he had won many glorious victories. His strength was in his hair (which was a badge or symbol of the presence of the Lord; his long hair untouched by razor signified his devotion to God, his dedication to service, his consecration to the God of heaven) but somehow he allowed the sacredness of the sign of God to escape him. Gradually he lost his reverence for it. Through his heroic deeds he captivated the hearts of many young maidens. In their presence he played with God's sign, growing careless and callous.

In every person there are two forces; one force that is trying to drive him down to the lowest hell and a force that is striving to lift him up to the highest heaven.

There are two master emotions—faith and fear. Fear is unbelief and because of fear a man gets his eyes off God, he loses his consecration and he is driven off course; in a sense he becomes unbalanced. A man becomes a plaything of his fears, often driven into orgies of passion and lust. Samson's sign was not magic. The spirit of God came upon him when he had faith. When Samson let his passions run wild, he, like any other man, became their slave. On the other hand, faith can conquer fear for it is stronger than fear. Faith is like light, it is a *force,* an *energy,* a *power.* Faith is stronger than fear as light is stronger than darkness. Darkness is not an energy, it has no life, no power. Turn on the light and you banish darkness but turn on darkness and the light keeps shining. You can't put light out by turning on darkness. The only way you can put those lights out here tonight is to turn them out or through a shortage, a power failure or a broken connection. Isn't that right?

Light comes from an energy called electricity. Darkness does not come from any such life-giving force or created power. Fear is like darkness, it has no power over our faith. It comes when faith is turned off. It controls us only as we do not use our faith. "Without faith it is impossible to please God." Without faith we have no locks on the door to keep fear out. When we live without faith fear comes in unbidden, makes itself welcome, takes control of our lives, drives us, frustrates us, torments us, binds us, makes us miserable, scatters our energy, breaks down our resistance, chills our bloodstream, and tears us all to pieces. But the moment you turn your faith on—the moment you look up and believe God and have faith in Jesus Christ—faith drives fear out of your heart, even as light drives darkness out of a room. Just as darkness can never return as long as you keep the light on, so fear can never come into your heart as long as you keep your faith and keep believing God. Do you believe that tonight? If you do, say, "Amen!"

CHAMPIONS CAN BE TEMPTED

Samson allowed himself to fall in love with a beautiful, wicked, young woman. His parents pleaded with him. They urged him not to go to Delilah but he felt because he had God's presence—this power, this sign of God—that he would not get in any danger; anyway, he could go pretty far without anything happening to him. That is where he made his fatal mistake.

I heard a story one time that has lived with me since I heard it. In the days of the wild west, when new frontiers were being opened, there was a particularly dangerous road that wound through the mountains and they were trying to hire a driver who would be careful enough not to wreck the stagecoach and endanger the passengers' lives. When they were hiring drivers they asked each man what his qualifications were. Some boys stepped up and were telling what good drivers they were, how well they could drive and how close to the edge they could drive without turning the stagecoach over. One young boy was standing back and when he heard them, he said, "Well, there's no use for me to apply," and he turned to walk off when the man in charge said, "Wait a minute, son. If I hired you what kind of driver would you be?" He said, "Mister, if you hired me I'd see how far *away from the edge* I could drive."

Men and women, it is not how close we can live to the world without getting seared and burned and hurt, no! It is how far *away* from the world we can live and keep God in our souls! If you have ever felt the presence of God, if at any time in your life you have had the experience where God touched you, or you felt Him in any remarkable way, then remember, that is the most sacred thing that ever happened to you. That is the thing that you should reverence and place your highest esteem upon. You should love above everything else, the *touches of God* upon your life. Yet many of us have had those touches of Christ upon us but we are selling our souls, our birthrights.

Dr. Sproull was telling me today about a young woman who was saved in our Norfolk, Virginia, meeting a year and a half ago and the following day she came to his afternoon meetings and went to the altar, knelt and asked him to have a prayer for her. When he knelt down to pray with her she looked up and said, "Brother Sproull, I'm a miserable woman today."

Dr. Sproull said, "What is wrong?"

She said, "Last night I went back in the prayer room and knelt and I found peace for my soul. I thought I had conquered this thing in me that had been driving me. This morning I committed adultery! Tonight I'm miserable." I wouldn't wonder. The very night before she had felt the presence of God. She had not kept its sacredness more than twelve hours. There is something wrong with people who do not reverence the presence of God.

Samson, the champion, felt like he could go the limit. He could do it and it wouldn't hurt him. That is the way everybody else feels. Everybody who has lost his soul felt like he wouldn't lose it. No one could convince him that he was going to lose it. Why, there are people who are not afraid of poison snakes. They say a poisonous snake won't bite. You are not going to tell me that, I know a poisonous snake will bite. I know that.

How many of you remember the story of the woman on the west coast who recently had a house full of snakes and she was known the world over as a lover of snakes? She had the most poisonous reptiles in captivity and would allow them to coil around her arm and would display them to her guests. She said, "They won't bite, they will not harm me."

One day when she was in the house alone she picked up one of the snakes she had made a pet and it sank its fangs in her arm and she died before anyone could get to her.

Yes, neighbor, snakes will bite and their poison will kill! You fool with sin and it will destroy you. Sin will blast your hopes, fire your passions, destroy your character, mark your soul, torment your mind and drive you to a devil's hell—not only in eternity, but you will live in hell every step that you take on this earth! There is only one way to handle sin and the devil and that is by God's power, resisting him in Jesus' name! There is complete victory over sin to that man or woman who will practice faith in God.

Samson played with God's sign. He had no reverence for it any longer and he teased his lover, trying to gain her favor so he could satisfy his lusts.

Why would a man allow himself to have lusts? The only reason any man ever commits adultery or any woman commits adultery, is because they want to do it; they allow themselves to be maneuvered into a place where they can't help it.

A man said to me, "I couldn't help it." You couldn't help it because you didn't want to help it. You did not consider life a sacred thing. You held no reverence for a human being.

I witnessed a tragedy in the home of two friends of mine recently. I suppose I will remember it forever. A fine young man, 35 years old, manager of a great corporation, carried on an affair for six months with one of the girls in the front office before they were caught. They called on me for prayer, asking me to "do something" for them. They thought my prayers would reach down and lift them out of it as though they had never sinned. It is true God hears my prayers and many have found new hope through my prayers but no man's prayers can save you until you hate your sins and want real victory. "Whatsoever a man soweth, that shall he also reap."

The young man said to me, "This girl was always after me. I tried to move her back in the inner office eight times and she wouldn't move."

I said, "I could have moved her. If I had been her boss I could have moved her back in the inner office!"

Later I talked to the girl and she told me a similar story. How did it all happen? Because neither one of them respected the image of God in each other.

You are made in God's image, in the likeness of the Creator. You have no right to despoil the image of God in the soul of another person! You have no right. God made that soul in the image and likeness of the Almighty and we ought to respect each other. A boy should help a girl if she is weak. A young girl came in our line one night and with tears said, "Brother Roberts, something possesses me when I get in the company of a boy and I allow him to use my body, pray that God will take it out of me." Millions could pray that prayer if they were honest enough to pray it. She realized that there was something within her spirit tormenting her and she wanted God's help. God did help her.

If a young woman is weak in the company of a boy that boy should respect the image of God in her soul; he owes her his strength to protect her and to help her keep her virtue. Every girl owes the boy seeking nothing but her flesh, her strength to strengthen him and to help him overcome that thing in his life.

We are losing the sacredness of life. There is not much reverence among humanity anymore. Women do not care how they sit, how they dress, in fact they dress so that men's passions will be stirred and then often cry when men seek what virtue they have left. Women, there's a hell for people like you and you are in that hell now for you will never go to the real hell until that hell comes in you in this world. Tomorrow night I'm preaching on "The Hell That Begins Here, And the Heaven That Begins Here," you will never go to hell until hell comes in you. You will never go to heaven until heaven comes in you. All that is settled down here.

And all the time that this young woman, the champion of Philistia, was battling with Samson she was battling with charms, cunning, intrigue and with passion and lust. And all that time her lords and rulers were putting silver in her hand. Don't ever forget, the boy who tries to steal your virtue despises you and will have no further use for you; the girl who tries to seduce you has no real love in her heart for you. We are so stupid. If we would only stop long enough to think and consider, how different things would be for us.

Samson thought he could win. Everyone else thinks he can win too but there has never been one yet who has won. There is only one way to win and that is to maintain a respect for the image of God in yourself and in all others.

Delilah was a champion. She was a highly paid champion, too. She was the champion of Philistia locked in a battle with the champion of the people of God. Samson came down and she cunningly set a trap for him and the trap was filled with her charms. His mother and father said, "Samson, don't you see what that girl is trying to do to you?" He said, "God's sign's in my life. I have *God's* presence. She'll never get me!"

Twelve months ago I received a telephone call from a minister. He said, "Oral, may I come to see you?"

I said, "Is this the minister that I knew when I was a small boy?"

He said, "Yes. Oral I helped pray for you when you were healed of T.B., and when you were saved I was praying for you."

I remembered it.

"What's the matter Claude?" I asked.

"I've got to see you," he replied.

In two hours and a half he drove from Oklahoma City to Tulsa. He was sitting with his wife in front of our office in their new car. I went to the door and motioned them to come in and he came in with his wife. He looked like he hadn't slept in a month, his face was haggard and drawn. He was only about 40 years old, a man who knew how to preach and make money. He was a man with many talents.

I said, "What's the matter with you? What's wrong with your eyes?" They were bloodshot.

He said, "Oral, I let the devil trick me."

"What happened?"

"I allowed a girl to seduce me. For thirty days I still felt some of the presence of God and I thought God was sanctioning what I was doing and so I continued to live with her, and one morning when I got up I felt like there was a fire in my soul. Toward evening I was so tormented I thought there were a thousand demons in my room and the next day I couldn't eat and the following day I was almost a maniac. I didn't sleep for a whole week and could carry no food on my stomach.

"Oral, I'm nearly crazy! The reason I am here is that I heard your broadcast Sunday and I got a little hope. Oral, what can you do for me?"

You know, people, I have lost interest in sin. I love my wife, I love my babies, I love my God, I love my fellowman. I am not interested in hurting anyone because I can't hurt someone without hurting myself worse. I know that, and there are thousands of people who can't sleep this night and their food doesn't agree with them because they have touched the image of God in somebody's life.

I took this minister into my arms and prayed until his soul was restored. When his nerves had quieted he said, "Oral, I am free again but I keep thinking of the awful price I have paid for my sin."

NO AFFINITY BETWEEN THEM

When Samson got down to Delilah's house, she seduced him and he accepted her charms and one night while they were in the bed in each other's arms, she put her mouth to his ear and said, "Samson, do you love me?" He said he did and you know if you love someone you have a right to expect something in return.

She said, "If you love me," (she never would have said 'if' had she known he really loved her; false love tries to make the same claims as true love) and she said, "Samson, if you love me, tell me wherein your great strength lieth that you may be afflicted."

He said, "Delilah, if you'll take seven green withs and tie me up I'll be as weak as other men."

Do you know what he was saying? He was saying, "There's something in my life that gives me great strength and if you take it away I'll be like other people." Samson knew the secret of his strength. He knew that he was only an ordinary man. A lot of people have the idea that Samson was a superman but he was no taller than the ordinary man, his arms were no larger and his muscles were no stronger. The only distinguishing thing about Samson was the spirit of God; when God's hand was upon him, he became strong. When God was not with him he was like any *other* man. Delilah was paid to find out his secret so that he could be reduced to the level of ordinary men. Delilah had one purpose: she intended to reduce Samson from spiritual power to the lowest physical level, to pervert his sex drive.

She got him to sleep and motioned to the liers in wait and said, "Bind him with seven green withs." Then she shook him and said, "Samson, awake! The Philistines be upon thee!" He awoke and saw that he was bound. He shook himself and broke the green withs as though they were the thread of tow touched by the fire. Like a tigress Delilah sprang at him and said, "Samson, you said that you loved me, why have you mocked me?"

He said, "Listen, Delilah, if you take new ropes and bind

me . . ." You see, he was seeking to favor her and was playing with God's sign to do it. They bound him with new ropes but he broke them like they were thread.

Why was Delilah wanting to discover the secret of Samson's strength and why was Samson lying to her? Because neither one of them loved each other. They mutually distrusted each other. Take respect out of love and no marriage can survive, the marriage bed becomes a source of frustration and torment. That is why people who build their marriages on lust cannot be happy because God has so fixed the sex life that it cannot be tampered with. The only soul-satisfying experience that can be found in the sex life is through love, real love; take love out and it becomes a flesh affair. It soon loses its power to satisfy and men push women from them and women despise their mates. They divorce each other and seek other mates and in turn lose them in the whirl of sin. Love is the only basis where two people can become one.

Samson and Delilah not only did not respect each other but they had no faith in each other; there was no affinity between them for if Samson had loved Delilah he could have trusted her, he would have told her the truth. If Delilah had loved him she would not have sought the source of his strength to betray him to her people. Do you see that? There was mutual distrust. They were afraid of each other.

What does all this mean? It means that there is no fellowship between sin and righteousness, no fellowship between this world and the work of God! You cannot mix faith with human lust and keep faith in your heart. God is a wonderful creator. He has given us all the ingredients for a happy marriage and a happy home and a happy family. "Marriage is honourable and the bed undefiled," the Bible says, and "For this cause a man shall leave his father and mother and cleave only unto his wife, and they both shall be twain." There is a breath-taking unity, a blending of spirit in a marriage ordained in heaven and carried out on this earth, but you have to have faith in God to have this kind of happiness. You have to put God first and in putting God first you are really putting *yourself* first. In putting God first you are simply using those ingredients which God designed for your happiness. A lot of people feel that when they put God first they are allowing themselves to be dominated by God and that God is an austere kind of a being that forces His will upon men. No! Not even Jesus wanted his will when He could take the Father's will! When you see the glory, the beauty and the happiness of God's way, you will not want your will. You will honestly say, "Not my will but God's will be done!" Friends, I long since have lost any desire to have my way, my will—I want the way of God. Every time I have had my way I have been dissatisfied and grown weary of it. I finally became so unhappy that I was frustrated. But when I have taken the will of God, a few months later I would say, "Oh, I'm glad I did that! My, I'm glad I took God's way out!"

Samson and Delilah were young people who never should have taken the first kiss, never should have lain in each other's arms; never should have allowed their passions to be stirred. Each man has control over his own passions and each woman has control over her own passions. Whatever is lacking God will supply if His help is wanted. But you must want God's power. You must seek His way. If you want God you must seek God. God isn't going to come to you automatically, God isn't going to give you His power and say, "Now no matter what you do you will forever have My power." The power of God is only *loaned* to people and it depends upon the way you obey Him whether or not you keep that power in your life.

I want to emphasize the fact that God does not force Himself on you. He is not seeking to dominate your life. God has rules of human happiness which, if you voluntarily live by, will bring you the fullest measure of inner power, peace of mind and prosperity. God is a good God. He wants only to bless your life. He is displeased only when you allow yourself to be dominated by lust and passion. God never takes anything from us unless we would be hurt by it. Should my little son take a knife in his hands to play with, I would stop him immediately because I know he would hurt himself. I want him to play but not with something dangerous.

God is angry when you take the snake of sin in your home and fondle it and play with it. When you say that it won't bite you or hurt you, God knows better. He knows it will poison and kill you! When you see that God is not an overmastering being, that He is not seeking to dominate you and to force Himself upon you, that He is available to bless you through your own choice—when you understand that—then you will love and want God in your life. You will want His good way.

THE BATTLE RAGES ON

Delilah saw Samson break the ropes and she said, "You mock me, Samson!"

"Oh," he said, "here's what to do, take the weaver's web and weave the seven locks of my head."

She did, and awoke him and said, "The Philistines are upon thee, Samson," and he awoke and carried the whole machine away with him. Delilah flew into a rage and cried, "Get out of my house! Get out of my chamber! Don't ever come back!"

Samson, that is good advice. You had better take it while you can.

She said, "You say you love me, you mock me. You've mocked me three times."

Samson wouldn't leave.

You go so far with passion and you never back out. There is a way to handle passion. Take God's way. You can do it if you want to do it!

Night after night as Samson lay in Delilah's arms, she said, "You don't love me! You don't love me!"

She vexed him and he said, "Oh Delilah, why must I prove my love to you every day?" You have to prove it to people who have no faith in you.

Some of you may find the key to your own unhappiness in your marriage tonight, if you will listen.

She vexed him but he did not have to be vexed; he could have gotten out of there if he had wanted out. God tempts no man. You cannot blame God tonight for any temptation you ever had. You can't do it, for the Bible says that, "God tempts no man." Every man is tempted when he is drawn away by his own lust or desire or when you let your own desire run wild. She vexed him continuously so that he was "vexed unto death." He realized he would have to give her up or tell her his secret.

Everyone dealing in sin reaches the point of no return, sooner or later. She goaded him and pushed him away from her but he would come back every time. Finally she said, "No! You cannot touch me again until you tell me!"

He said, "All right."

Oh Samson, don't tell her, don't tell her the secret of God!

He said, "I'll tell you. Sit down here by my side on the bed, please, Delilah. When I was a little child my mother told me a story. She said, 'Samson, you are God's child. An angel announced your birth . . .'"

"Yes, Samson, go on," Delilah said quickly.

"And, mother said the angel told her I was never to drink wine or to shave the seven locks of my head."

Delilah caught her breath and said, "Oh! And why is that, what does your *hair* have to do with it?"

He said, "Delilah, the sign of God is in my hair. My long hair is a symbol of my consecration to Him, it is the evidence that He is with me. As long as I keep the seven locks of my hair, the symbol of God's presence, I will have His power to defeat the enemies of the Lord God. If they were shaven off, I would be weak as other men." Not that his strength was in his hair, but his hair is a symbol of his consecration of God.

Delilah said, "Oh, I see, now Samson you relax, you're tired. You've had a heavy day, Samson, just lie down here and rest." When he lay down she ran out and said to the Philistines, "Come quickly. He's told me all in his heart." She went in and said, "Here Samson, lay your head in my lap, let me smooth your temples." Oh, when will men and women ever have any sense? When will they ever have wisdom? When will they ever see what they are getting into?

Samson went to sleep, and that night the barber crept in and shaved off the seven locks of his head. Next morning she shook him and said, "Samson! Samson! Awake! The Philistines are here!"

He awoke and shook his head, rubbed the sleep out of his eyes, got up, looked around and saw the Philistine soldiers with swords drawn surrounding him in a circle and he said, "I will shake myself as at other times." He drew up his arms and felt nothing! The power was gone! The spirit of the Lord did not come upon him. He said "No! No! Delilah! Delilah, you didn't, did you . . . no! No!"

She said, "Oh yes, I did."

He said, "Oh God, your spirit is gone from me. I am like other men. I have played the fool."

Samson dropped his hands to his side, saying, "All right, go ahead, take me. There's no use for me to fight against you, I have no power."

THE CONQUEROR OF SAMSON

Who is the conqueror of Samson? Not the soldiers of Philistia; not the young lion; not the gatepost of his enemy; not his own people, not even Delilah. He was conquered by his own compromise. Compromise conquered Samson. Why did he not resist? Because there is a moral law in a man's soul. When you violate your own conscience, when you take away that reverence, that sacredness of your faith in God— you know and every man knows there is no need to strike back. A violated conscience reduces the giant to a pigmy, the greatest man to the least.

THE PRISONER

They took him and put out his eyes. But they never put out Samson's eyes until he proved he couldn't see. He was not in darkness until the light of God went out in his own soul. They took him to prison. They hooked him up in the place of a mule and made him grind in the prison house of their god.

This is God's champion. This is Samson, the unconquerable. This is the boy whose birth the angels announced. This is the champion of God, blinded, sweaty, grinding at the mill, a prisoner in the prison house of Delilah's God.

Prisoner! No longer is he champion but a prisoner. Look at him. They dress him in a loin cloth, his hair is shaven to

his head, his eyes are put out and black rims circle the
place where his eyeballs once were; they hook him up to
the end of the tongue in the prison-house mill. There he
found a road already cut out for his feet. He didn't need
eyes to grind in this prison house. Round and round! Round
and round! Round and round!

Many of us are prisoners. Prisoners of worn-out creeds, of
antiquated theology, of custom and convention. We have
lost the joy of the Lord. We are prisoners, prisoners to somebody's creed and ideology; prisoners of our own worldly am-
bitions. Prisoners of lust and passion. Round and round we
go. We are not going anywhere, we have already been there.
We are grinding at the mill. Prisoners!

RECOVERING THE SIGN

Now, recovering the sign. One morning Samson is grinding. He is so tired. He is remembering his glory. He can't
see. That morning something keeps brushing across his
shoulder, something touches the back of his neck, he stops
and he says, "Oh God! My hair! My hair is growing again!"
The Bible said, "Howbeit his hair began to grow again after
he was shaven." As long as there is a God, there is a re-
course. Joyce Kilmer said, "Poems are made by fools like
me but only God can make a tree." He could have said,
"Poems are made by fools like me but only God can make
a *man's hair grow again!*" All this means God is still interested in those who have lost in the battle of life. Samson
was still champion, although a fallen one. God never forgets
those who once loved Him.

Samson cried, "My hair is growing again. God has thought
of me again."

How God loved Samson.

About that time he heard chains rattling on his door. Soldiers had come for him.

REBIRTH OF A CHAMPION

Now I want to tell you one of the most amazing stories of the Bible—the rebirth of a champion. When the soldiers opened the door he was grinding again. He did not mention that his hair was growing again. They came down the stairs and said, "All right Samson, you can stop your grinding now."

He said, "What do you want?"

One of them said, "I've been sent for you. The king has ordered me to bring you to our temple."

"What for?" Samson asked.

"This is our feast day, our day of glorious victory for the fatherland. You see, all the lords and ladies of Philistia have gathered at the temple of our god, Dagon, to celebrate our victory over you, our enemy. You are to make sport for them," the soldier said.

They released Samson, shoved him up the stairway. As they walked down the road to the temple of Dagon, Samson said, "Tell me about your temple, Philistine."

"It's a glorious temple, the most beautiful temple in the world. It is the temple of our god, Dagon."

"How is it built, Philistine?"

"Why," he said, "it is one of the wonders of the world! The whole structure is supported by two pillars."

"Are they close together?"

"Close enough for a man to stand between them."

Better shut your mouth, Philistine, you are driving nails in your own casket—a man's faith is coming back again.

God knows the vital weakness of your enemy. If you have

faith in God you will be shown that weakness, you will be given the secret of liberation. If you are bound by lust, God knows the one weakness of this enemy and will reveal it to you. If you are bound by liquor or some other vice God knows the way to victory. Thousands have sought God and found perfect deliverance.

When they brought Samson into the temple of Dagon, a great shout went up and they cried, "Honor Delilah! She hath conquered Samson, our enemy!" Delilah rose and took her bow. Some smart one said, "Bring out a young lion. I hear that he can slay a young lion with his own hands, bring one out." And they laughed. Someone said, "No, just turn Delilah loose on him, she knows how to conquer champions."

This time the champion doesn't desire Delilah, he is free from her. This time the champion *can see,* only his eyes are blind, that's all. He can see now a lot more clearly than he did when he had his eyes. This time the champion is humble, this time God is with him. Pretty soon they sent a little boy to keep him moving and this lad had him to walk in this place and that place. The great temple was full of the lords and ladies of Philistia. The old king was watching the spectacle with great sport and Delilah was mentally counting her silver that she had been paid for her conquest of the champion.

Pretty soon Samson leaned down and said, "Sonny boy, where are the two pillars that the temple is built on?"

"They're right over here, Samson."

"Son, if you'll take me over there, I'll pull this place down."

Only the little boy had faith enough to believe that Samson could pull the temple down. He said, "Right this way, Samson," and when he got over there where the pillars were, some smart aleck in the crowd said, "Ha! He's going to pull the temple down. Look at him, he's going to pull the temple down."

That is just exactly what he is going to do.

Samson stood between the pillars and he felt for them in his blindness and he got his arms around them and somebody said, "Everybody look! The old champ will pull the temple down!"

For an answer Samson bowed his head, then raised it to heaven and said,

"Oh Lord God, remember me just this once. I pray Thee oh God, just once more let me feel Thy power again. Oh, Lord God, this time may I feel Thy power, not to play with God's sign, but this time that I may pull down Dagon's house. Please God, just one more time!"

The Philistines looked at him with fascination, nobody moved, they scarcely breathed. All of a sudden Samson felt a little tremor in his body, a sensation like a fierce wind surged through him. It was the spirit of the living God. A champion was being reborn.

"Son, get out of here, get out of here son, run for your life son, get out now!" Samson whispered to his little escort.

While everybody was deathly still he put his arms around those pillars and bent forward and when he did the roof trembled, the walls crumbled. Someone screamed, "Look! Look! His God has come back to him. His God is with him again. Get out of here! Everybody run!"

The old king turned deathly pale but could not move. Three thousand Philistines sat in horror, spectators at a drama of God's power.

Samson moved again, the spirit of God ran up and down the walls and cracked them. Then three thousand voices

began to scream, "My God! Our God! Get me out of here."
While they screamed, Samson pulled the temple down, it
came crumbling down on its foundations, rock upon rock,
mortar upon mortar, dust upon dust, Philistine upon Philistine!

Where is Samson? There he is. He is buried beneath the
debris, his body is crushed. All you can see is his head. See
him there. He's looking up. His lips are moving. What is he
saying? I hear him now. He is saying, "Mine eyes have seen
the glory of the Lord." A champion is reborn!

Every head bowed please.

WHY I BELIEVE JESUS IS COMING SOON AND WHAT HIS COMING WILL MEAN TO YOU AND ME

Scripture Text: Luke 1:11–37; 2:10–12; 2:25–38
I Thessalonians 4:13–18

three | Why I Believe Jesus Is Coming Soon and What His Coming Will Mean to You and Me

There are preliminaries to every event of major importance and the very things that precipitated the first coming of Christ are going to bring about His second return. I want you for a moment to think with me along an entirely different line of thinking about His soon return. Did you know that the timetable of God is perfect and never gets out of step, or tune or time? The timetable of God is arranged by the Lord Almighty and at the exact moment that God has planned the return of His Son, he *will* return without fail.

Jesus could have been born at only one certain time in the world's history. He could have been born only on one specific day and He was born at that time. The Bible said He was to be born in Bethlehem. The young woman who was bearing Him as a baby did not live in Bethlehem, she had made no plans to go to Bethlehem, and during the long months of waiting to bear His humanity—God did not have her to take one step toward Bethlehem until just a few hours prior to the time Jesus was to be born. Then Mary learned only a short time before the time that she was to go. She made the hazardous trip there in the nick of time.

God never hurries, God doesn't have to hurry because

God is a God of faith. The only people who hurry are those who are afraid. They are bound by fear and they feel that unless they do certain things their life is going to turn out wrong, but God knows and he moves at the proper time in men's lives. He knows what is coming to pass. If we live by faith, we will know His will for us; we will never become frustrated, or tormented by inner conflicts or driven by festering fears. We will conquer through our faith in Jesus Christ of Nazareth. If you believe it tonight, say Amen!

Now, the world had to be in a certain condition for the birth of Jesus. It has to be in a certain condition for His return. Here are the remarkable and incredible things that had to take place for Jesus' birth. You will be thrilled to the depths of your soul tonight as you hear them. Did you know that four things had to be in operation for Jesus to be born? One of them was a universal language; another was universal peace; another, universal taxation and the fourth was a universal network of highways. The Greeks gave the first—a universal language. When Alexander the Great conquered, he also Hellenized the world, that is, he carried Greek culture with him everywhere he went and the Greek language (which is the most beautiful and expressive of all human languages) became the language of commerce and was understood by the people all over the world. They had no press or radio, or television; no communication system in the time that Jesus Christ was born on this earth. News had no way of traveling like it does today, but in a matter of days the news of Jesus' birth traveled to the far corners of the earth because of these four things. When the Romans conquered Greece, they retained the Greek language. Everybody understood the Greek language so that when Jesus was born and they announced it, everybody could understand in the same language, that a Saviour was born in Bethlehem.

Then, there was peace in the world. True, it was an enforced peace but there was peace at any rate, and the sword was not lifted up in Jesus' time, in war.

There was a universal network of highways. The Romans are famous for the great highways they built and over there in Italy and North Africa and in various parts of the Mediterranean world, there remain yet parts of those old, ancient hard-surfaced roads. In the days when Jesus was born, travel was easy.

Then, remarkably enough, there came a universal taxation. Now what's so incredible about that? Simply this: When God was ready for Jesus to be born, Mary lived in Nazareth, yet the Bible said (hundreds of years before) he would be born in Bethlehem. How would God get Mary to Bethlehem in time for the birth of Jesus? In the heart of Caesar Augustus there came the thought of taxing the whole world. Now when the taxing laws were to be applied in Judea, the people were taxed in their own home towns, where their fathers were originally registered. So Mary, being of the house of David, had to go back to the home of her father David which was Bethlehem. So the universal taxation came at the propitious time. God had reckoned for His Son to be born and Mary got there just in time; in fact someone might say that she was too late because there was no room for them in the inn but God did not mind, for one of the signs that the babe born of Mary would be Jesus was made clear by the angel who said: ". . . this shall be a sign unto you, ye shall find the babe wrapped in swaddling clothes and lying in a manger." The baby Jesus would be found lying in a manger. No other baby would qualify. Oh the signs of God!

THESE PEOPLE KNEW

Exactly ten groups of people or angels were warned by God either directly or informed through premonitions about Jesus' birth. The first one was an angel, Gabriel, one of the archangels of God. God said, "Gabriel, you have two missions to perform: You are to announce the birth of My Son, Jesus, but you must also announce the birth of His forerunner for My Son must have the way prepared for Him and you shall go to the house of a certain minister, a priest of God, whose wife is old and barren, who cannot bear children. He has been in prayer; speak to him and tell him that I will visit his home with a child. Six months later, go to a young virgin named Mary in Nazareth and tell her she is to bear the Son of God."

One day, Zacharias was ministering before the Lord when the angel Gabriel appeared and stood by his side. Zacharias was troubled and afraid. The angel said "Fear not, Zacharias, for the Lord is visiting you, he has heard your prayer and now your wife Elizabeth shall conceive a child in her old age and he shall bring great joy to your heart for he shall prepare the way of the Lord."

"Why," Zacharias said, "how can this be?" He was full of unbelief and the angel said, "You will be struck dumb until the child is born!" Think of that! He lost the power of speech because of his unbelief.

Six months later the same angel came to a young woman in Nazareth and said, "Hail thou that art highly favoured of God! Mary, the Holy Spirit shall overshadow thee and thou shalt conceive a child in thy womb and He shall be the Son of the Most High! He shall be called the Son of God, even Jesus!"

She said, "Why, I know not a man, how can this be?" And

the angel Gabriel said, ". . . for with God, nothing shall be impossible," and she said, "Behold, here is thy handmaiden, do unto her as the Lord pleases." So the great preliminary had begun. Here are the first three who were told: Gabriel, Zacharias and Mary. Then a carpenter was told, just a plain carpenter over in Nazareth. One day the angel said to him, "Joseph, do not be afraid to take this girl to be your wife for that which is conceived in her is the Son of God, and you shall call His name Jesus, for He shall save His people from their sins." So Joseph was not afraid to take Mary as his wife.

Then somebody else was told. In the East, hundreds of miles from Judea, wise men were studying the sky when they saw in the heavens a new star, the star of Christ. It was a star designating royalty and they said, "A king is to be born. That is a star of majesty, of royalty! Let us follow it!" Here is the strange thing about their following the star: they could not travel by day because the star did not shine in the day-time, they followed the star only at *night*. They traveled at night over mountains, through valleys, across great bodies of water, through mountain vastnesses, but they came plod-ding on following that star. They knew it was the star of a new king that was coming upon the earth.

But now something else happened. While the wise men were coming, the Roman legions came into Judea with their order to tax the people. Mary and Joseph came to Bethle-hem. When they arrived there was no room for them in the inn and they had to take Mary to a stall where the baby Jesus was born, and wrapped in swaddling clothes, and laid in a manger. At that exact moment on the hillsides of Judea obscure shepherds, unknown to the great priests of God were tending their flocks at night. Angels filled the air and said, "Fear not, for unto you is born this day in the city of David a Saviour, which is Christ the Lord, and this shall be a sign unto you, you shall find him wrapped in swaddling clothes and lying in a manger." So these shepherds, wondering, said, "Let us go see." When they arrived they found the Holy Child, Jesus. A little later the wise men arrived and presented their gifts of gold, frankincense and myrrh, showing their worship and adoration of royalty, Jesus the King of Kings and Lord of Lords!

Later, Mary and Joseph brought the baby Jesus to the temple of God in Jerusalem. There lived in Jerusalem a man, just and devout, waiting for the consolation of Israel and the Holy Ghost was upon him. The Holy Ghost said, "Simeon, you will not die until you have seen the Lord's Christ." Isn't that a wonderful thing? There was one man in Jerusalem who knew he wouldn't die until he saw the Lord. He wasn't afraid he would have an accident, he wasn't afraid he would die prematurely, the Holy Spirit had said, "You will not die, Simeon, until. . . ." So Simeon waited, knowing. The Bible said, ". . . he was waiting for the consolation of Israel." There are some people alive in this audience tonight who may not die until they have seen Jesus Christ coming again. When you realize that tonight, it ought to stir the very depths of your soul. So when Mary and Joseph brought the Holy Child, Jesus, into the temple of God, Simeon came in and saw the baby and the Holy Spirit said, "That is the baby!" He rushed over and without a word took the baby from Mary's arms and held the child up and said "Now, Lord, lettest thy servant depart in peace for mine eyes have seen the glory of the Lord, the salvation of thy people Israel." Oh glory to His Name!

At that exact instant there was an old, old woman—over a hundred years old—who came in the temple of God and saw the baby Jesus and said, "That is the Christ, the Son of God." She too took the child and blessed him and spoke of him to all those who looked for redemption in Israel. Now here is a combination of circumstances, here is the incredible moving of the miraculous spirit of Almighty God—preliminaries, things that had to take place, all of them shaping up to one end: the birth of a baby who was wrapped in swaddling clothes and who was to become King of Kings and Lord of Lords.

So Jesus was born and grew up to be thirty years of age. But he did not begin to preach until John the Baptist had prepared the way for Him. Thirty years had passed by and out in the wilderness, God's last messenger is to be informed about him. John did not know his exact mission on earth although he must have had a general idea. He knew he was to prepare the way of the Lord but he did not know who the Lord was. The other groups, or individuals, had been warned and had played their part. There was a humble wilderness preacher who lived in the woods near the Jordan river, out there alone—who had been born for such a time as this. But how will he know? Just the way God informs *us* in these last days. The Holy Spirit said to him, "One of these days you are going to be preaching and there shall come one in the crowd whose face is fairer than the sons of men. He is the Lord's Christ, and when you see the Holy Spirit descending upon him in the form of a dove you will know that he is the Son of God. That is the sign."

Notice now the triple-sign of Jesus; first, he was wrapped in swaddling clothes and placed in a manger; second, the star of Jesus which the wise men had to follow and third, the holy dove, or the Holy Spirit in the form of a dove. God moves by signs and without a sign God does not move. "For these signs shall follow them that believe; in My Name they shall cast out demons, they shall heal the sick," bringing deliverance to humanity.

Do you believe it? Say Amen!

Paul spoke of the mighty signs and wonders performed through his ministry, ". . . not with enticing words of man's wisdom," he said, "but by mighty signs."

So this wilderness preacher was given his orders. One day he was preaching at Jordan. A vast crowd was listening. It was a day of great revival and the power of God was being poured out—crowds were flocking to hear this man of God, when Jesus walked up. He said nothing. But John saw Him. Jesus walked up to him and said, "Baptize me."

"Why," John said, "I have need to be baptized of Thee—not You of me!"

Jesus said, "Suffer us to fulfill all righteousness (go ahead and baptize me)."

So he baptized Him and when He came up out of the water the heavens opened and the Holy Ghost descended in the form of a dove and John cried, "Behold the Lamb of God that taketh away the sin of the world!"

Gabriel, Zacharias, Mary, Simeon, Anna, the Wise Men, the shepherds, Joseph, and John the Baptist all knew. They played their part in a drama that ended in the birth and ministry of our Lord Jesus. We too, are raised up of God in these last days—God's hand is upon us. Some of us will cry, "Behold the Lord cometh! Behold the Lord cometh!"

THREE THINGS JESUS DID

Jesus began His public ministry. He did three major things. Jesus is not hard to understand if you're simple enough to understand Him, but complicated folks can't understand Him because complicated folks can't understand simple things. Jesus was always begging people to be like children, to be childlike in their understanding, not to go off on some tangent and fail to understand how God moves.

First, *Jesus gave a new interpretation of God.* The world was dominated by fear. In their rebellion against God they had become afraid. In fear they lifted up their hands against their fellow man. No one trusted anybody. When Jesus came they distrusted His mission so that he had to give that classic text "The Son of Man is not come to destroy men's lives but to save them." He had to set them at ease—to realize that He had not come with a sword or with regal power to destroy them but to save them as a lamb slain from the foundation of the world. The old interpretation of God presented Him as austere and harsh; a God of justice (not mercy): He put sickness upon people such as blindness, consumption, deafness, even crippling their bodies so that the more one was afflicted the more godly one was. (Jesus healed a man who had been born blind. His fellows had said he had been born in sin, that he was blind either through his own sins or the sins of his parents.) This interpretation they had was absolutely false and unreal. Jesus gave a new picture of God: He is a loving God; a good God; that all the good and perfect gifts cometh down from God. To prove this Jesus went about doing good, healing all who were oppressed of the devil for God was with Him. He went among their sick, not handing out other diseases but healing the diseases which they had. He went among them casting out devils and leaving the people with joy—great joy—so that they were astonished and said, "We've never seen it on this order before." Wherever He went there was great joy in that land, people flocked to hear Him; they wanted only to touch the hem of his garment. "And as many as touched him were made every whit whole." They got a new idea of God, that He is closer than hands and feet; that He is not outside our troubles; not removed from our diseases, but within all of them like He was in the fiery furnace with the three Hebrew children as the Fourth Man, robbing the fire of its sting; subduing the crackling flames and bringing them forth to glorious victory.

People received new hope. They could sleep better at night. They could do their work a whole lot better, they had a new spring in their step, a new light in their eye, a new love and faith in God. They felt they had something to live for again. Men and women, when you get this interpretation of Christ it will put new life in you, you will work for the Lord and face your fellow men with new hope, new courage and new faith but if you don't understand the way He works you will be whipped, defeated in life.

Jesus gave a new interpretation.

Second, He said, "If I go away, I will send you another comforter." There are two comforters, Jesus and the Holy Ghost. He said, ". . . it is expedient for you that I go away, if I go not away the comforter (which is the Holy Ghost) will not come, but if I go I will send Him unto you." This is one of the most remarkable things in the whole Bible. It shows the great love of God for us. There was a very deep attachment the disciples had for the physical presence of Jesus and I think if everyone here had his highest desire tonight, he would rather see Jesus in the flesh than to have anything in the world! This is because we have the idea the physical presence of the Lord is more real, more applicable to our needs, more within the realm of our being helped, than it is to have the "other comforter." But Jesus tells us the truth, he said ". . . it is expedient for you that I go away." If it had been best, Jesus would have remained in the flesh, but he knew that if he had remained in the flesh millions of us would never have gotten within fifty miles of Him because if Jesus Christ were in this place millions and millions of people would come to this city just for the privilege of touching the hem of His garment.

I went to a little North Carolina town, Whiteville, with a population of 3,800 people. I went there for a few days' rest in the home of Lee Braxton, the radio director of Healing Waters broadcast. He prevailed on me to speak on Sunday night at their church uptown and I consented to do it with the understanding that it would not be publicized or announced in the newspapers. But somehow the news got around. When I got in there that night (driving in from Lake Waccamaw), and I got there before sundown, the police department had roped off the main street and cars were parked a half mile in either direction from the church and there were more people around the church and in the streets than there were in the city of Whiteville—over 4,000 people were there to hear me preach that night and to be healed. How they knew I would be there, I do not know! The answer is that people are so desperate, they need God, they need healing and if they know someone has God's commission to heal the sick and to perform miracles in His wonderful name, they will come any distance and do anything to receive deliverance through the power of God. They did in Jesus' time, they will do it today. If Christ were here in the flesh you and I would not get within a hundred miles of Him because the limits of His physical presence are so severe. He could only be in one place at a time. He could only take one step at a time. He did not vanish in space as long as He was in the physical flesh. I know He had that power after He rose from the dead but as a man, before He died, He had to walk as other men walked and He used the same principles of faith that are available to every man, woman and child today.

So, He said, ". . . it is better for you if I go away because if I go I will send you another comforter." Now he says, "I am your present comforter but I will send you another one co-equal with me in the Godhead, and this comforter is the Holy Ghost." There is God the Father, God the Son and God the Holy Ghost, three in one, one in three, neither separated from the other—all co-equal with each other. Does that sound mysterious? It is. Just like it sounds, it is mysterious. But He said, "I will send you another One who is the same in the Godhead as I am and He will come to you even as I am with you now, with this exception, I will put Him 'in' you; He is 'with' you now but when I go away I will put him in you, where they cannot get their hands on Him to crucify Him like they will crucify me. I will put Him beyond the realm of crucifixion. He shall be *in* you."

Now there is a vast difference in having something with you and having something in you. Every child of God has the Holy Spirit with him, you cannot be saved without the Holy Spirit because the Holy Spirit saves a man. You are drawn by the spirit of God to the Father. The Bible says—you are "sanctified by the Holy Ghost." So then the Holy Ghost, the "other Comforter" Jesus promised to send after he went away both saves and sanctifies before He personally comes in to abide with us as our Comforter in the Baptism of the Holy Ghost.

We had a Nazarene minister in Tulsa who came to these great meetings. Under the full gospel ministry of Pastor Steve Pringle (and myself) he received the baptism of the Holy Ghost. He was strangely moved by it. I heard him preach his first sermon after he received the Holy Ghost. He was a new man, he preached with more power, more glory, more inspiration. He said in this sermon, "People, I'm amazed at myself. I had the Holy Spirit 'with' me all time (I thought I had the baptism and I found out I was only sanctified) and now I have Him 'in' me, and to think that I thought there was no difference between having Him with me and having Him in me until now." He said, "I used to work on public jobs and I took my lunch *with* me but at noon I put it *in* me, I have had the blessed Holy Ghost with me ever since my conversion, but now I have Him *in* me, and that makes all the difference in the world."

I want to ask the ten thousand people gathered before me tonight this question: "Have ye received the Holy Ghost since ye believed?"

Some of you say, "Brother Roberts, I have not even heard of the Holy Spirit." That is because your preacher won't preach it, your preacher doesn't believe it. If the preachers believed in the Holy Ghost which the Bible teaches, ninety percent of their members would believe in it. One of the chief reasons you church folks don't believe in it is because you do not have the intestinal fortitude to stand up and face your pastor and tell him he is wrong, you are cowards, you are not made out of the right kind of stuff, you are not listening to the right preacher, you are not attending the right church.

I had a pastor write to me and he said, "You have no right to tell my people to stay away from my church just because I don't preach the Holy Ghost."

I have every right in the world for if you do not attend the church that believes in the Holy Ghost you probably never will receive the baptism of the Holy Ghost. If you fail to receive this glorious Bible experience you will miss the experience which the disciples received on the day of Pentecost. You will fail to receive the tremendous *power* the comforter bestows, and you will not have the glorious "comfort" of the Holy Ghost. I would fail God and you if I did not urge you to go where you can hear about and receive the Holy Ghost.

But now to you people who have had the Holy Ghost and have not been yielded vessels in His hands I ask this question: "Have you been refilled since you leaked out?"

It is the duty of every person to examine his own soul, his thinking, his theology. We must receive the baptism of the Holy Ghost and once we have this experience we must continue to live holy, consecrated lives so that we will be instruments through which the power of the Holy Ghost flows to deliver this generation.

You should not try to live a christian life without the Holy Ghost, and you should not stop until you receive the Holy Ghost, and with that power do exploits in His name. There may be a few things you don't like about the Holy Ghost, that is where you are wrong. You may not like the fact that when you receive the Holy Spirit you speak with tongues, but who are you to order God around? You ought to be ashamed of yourself. You say, "But my pastor's a great man, and he said there wasn't anything to it." Many ministers are denying their people the knowledge of the Holy Ghost. They are missing God and causing their people to miss God. I love the Holy Ghost. It is only through the power of the Holy Ghost that God's healing power pours through my life. I owe what I have to the experience of Pentecost. I have been saved and sanctified by the blood of Christ. I knew that I was holy by His power, but I knelt in the straw of an old-fashioned Holy Ghost camp meeting, raised my hands and said "God, baptize me with the Holy Spirit, give me power to deliver my generation," I did not care what the world thought, I wanted the power. Do you know what convinced me? I needed this power. The scripture says, "Ye shall receive power after that the Holy Ghost is come upon you," not before He comes, but after; not when you're saved; not when you're sanctified, but after the Holy Ghost comes upon you. With my hands up, praising God, the Holy Ghost *fell* upon me, a light engulfed me and I began to speak in a new language, God filled me with the Holy Ghost and His power came into my life; a power I had never known before. And if you have the nerve to criticize me for that then I shall not be disappointed nor discouraged, because you are not mocking me, you are mocking the God who baptized me with the Holy Ghost.

Preachers, have you received the Holy Ghost since you believed?

Preachers, have you been refilled since you leaked out?

There is only one sad note I have to say about the Holy Spirit's work in our lives. Some of us do not use wisdom with our zeal. We have become odd and have allowed some people to misuse this experience in fleshly demonstrations. I am sorry that is true, but it is. But there will always be people like that. Always. But, neighbor, I shall not give up my Holy Ghost experience, not I, because I intend to treasure the gold, the glory, the beauty of the genuine experience of the baptism of the Holy Ghost and fire.

A wealthy businessman visited me. He came in my home and said, "Reverend Roberts, I heard you preach the other night, and you're a great preacher." When he began to brag on me I knew something was coming.

"Young man, you're going to take this world by storm."

He said, "I've never heard anything like it, young man, I was thrilled, I was lifted up. God did something for me through your preaching. I saw other people blessed, too, they scarcely moved at all while you preached."

"Yes?" I said.

"But, young man, you're off on the wrong track a little bit."

"Yes?"

"You emphasized the Holy Ghost too much."

"Oh?"

"If you quit that the nominal churches would support you then," he said while he looked straight at me.

The source of the power in my life that attracts the multitudes to these meetings, resulting in over 50,000 souls being saved each year and other thousands being healed through my humble prayers is in the emphasis I *do* place on the Holy Spirit. I cannot and will not compromise with the so-called nominal churches. They are officially, ecclesiastically and diametrically opposed to the baptism of the Holy Ghost through which God has given me His wondrous power to lead men to Christ and bring His deliverance to them. The nominal churches—their preachers and people—must change their attitude toward the Holy Ghost. The time has come when *all* of us must re-think the experience of the upper room on Pentecost morning.

The third thing that Jesus did: He said, "If I go away, I will come again." He said that he would return. He went away suddenly and the angels said he would return in like manner—suddenly. So, He gave a new interpretation of God; He promised another comforter and third, He said He would return suddenly.

All of these things had their beginning when God said, "Gabriel, go on your mission. Tell Zacharias, tell Mary. . . ." Christ was born, began His ministry, preached, healed the people and gave men a new picture of God, when he gave the Holy Spirit, whom he called "another comforter" and said he was returning suddenly. This is exactly where we are on God's timetable: We are expecting his sudden return.

Now, there are three major preliminaries that are going on this very moment concerning His second coming. When I give them to you I think you will realize what I mean when I say I expect Him to come any moment, day or night.

Listen now. Did you know that an entire nation is on the move across the face of the earth right now? Did you know that the Jews are returning to Palestine in unprecedented numbers? And that since 1918, they have multiplied thirty times? They had 50,000 Jews in Palestine during World War I; today they have one and one-half million—an increase of three thousand percent! Thirty times the population of 1918! If America had grown the past thirty years like Palestine has grown, do you know how many people this country would have? Instead of 150,000,000 we would have four and one-half billion! Imagine that tonight. When you see the fig tree putting forth its leaves—its buds, then know ye that your redemption draweth nigh.

The Jews are returning in unbelief. They may not know it yet but they are returning according to God's timetable. Already their flag flies the high seas. They *will* rebuild the temple and in that temple antichrist will stand. He will break his covenant with unbelieving Jews by demanding them to worship him in their temple. When they refuse he will begin his unholy massacre called in the Bible "The Abomination of Desolation." When Christ comes back on earth, a nation shall be born in a day. Many of them shall flee the wrath of antichrist, hiding in the mountain fortresses of Palestine and will be ready to believe on Jesus when he comes back. This is the first preliminary: the returning of the Jews. An unseen force is pulling them back to their ancestral home. In all the nations of the earth thousands of Jews feel the strange urge to go back. Big four-motored airplanes are carrying them even from remote areas. Isaiah saw these planes flying as eagles. He saw them coming in from the isles of the sea, he saw them coming from the far corners of the earth. A nation is marching across the earth because Jesus is coming soon.

The second preliminary is the strange premonition. Once again the Simeons in their just and devout lives are hearing the Holy Spirit speak to them. It won't be long now. It won't be long.

There are people in this audience tonight who have had a touch from God. I heard that one of the cooperating pastors had something unusual happen to him just recently and he is not the same man anymore. What does it mean? Practically every sincere minister in the world tonight has the same testimony, something is happening to us. There are humble people in this audience who are not preachers; you are not in the front row; you are not in the amen corner of the church, but you love God and God has been strangely dealing with your soul. What is it? It is a premonition. That is what Simeon had—a premonition that he would be alive to see the Lord's Christ face to face. I am just as certain tonight that God raised me up to help prepare the way for the catching away of His bride as I know my name is Oral Roberts. I know that. The past few weeks I have felt so strange. I have even curtailed some of my outside interests. I am a busy man. My mind is fertile and I have to reach out into many fields of human endeavor to satisfy it but I have the strangest feeling that I should concentrate on telling everyone I can reach: Jesus is coming soon. I don't want anything to distract me from this task. I know that if I get interested in something that might cause me to miss the coming of the Lord, I would be the most miserable wreck who ever walked the earth. Mrs. Roberts and I are very careful with our children these stressful days. We are having special prayers with them every morning and night. We are carefully reading the Bible to them, buying Bible books for them and telling our children that Jesus is coming soon. My children know that Christ is coming.

Listen folks, if you are mixed up in something that casts

a shadow over your soul, quit it tonight, stop it! Get rid of
it! If you are mixed up in something that is breaking your
fellowship with God, stop it tonight. Oh people, if you miss
the coming of the Lord you will miss the greatest thing in
your life. Don't miss it, don't miss the coming of the Lord.
People, if you have to go back and apologize to somebody,
get on your knees with tears and say, "Please forgive me."
Do it! Do it in this meeting, go back and apologize. Do
anything under the sun to get your soul ready for the coming
of Jesus of Nazareth. Some of you have old back debts you
have not paid. Make immediate plans to take care of them.
Some of you are robbing God in tithes and offerings—start
tithing now. Start back to church; teach your children right;
have thanks at the table every time you eat a meal; look up
to God when you leave your home to go to work, ask God
to watch over you that day and if He should come that day,
please to take you with Him! Talk to Him like that! Let us
not miss the coming of the Lord. Let us go with Jesus. Everybody say, "Amen," if you believe that tonight!

Listen now, a nation is on the move, and many feel divine
premonitions. The third preliminary is a world-wide revival.
John the Baptist is preaching again! Have you heard *John*
preach lately? I have. You are hearing one of them tonight.
Who is John the Baptist? Those people that are energized
by the Holy Spirit through whom God is saying, "Prepare
the way of the Lord." That is why I am preaching tonight.
I have a message from God. I am pushing a Holy Ghost bull-
dozer tonight! I am coming through the wilderness of man's
sin preaching for deliverance, and that men shall know
that Jesus is coming soon. If you will listen to me there will
not be even one of you unprepared—everyone will be ready.
That is worth more than houses and lands or silver and gold.
People, quit pinching your dollars when it comes to God's
service. Now is the time to give to missions. *Now is the time*

to give to missions. Now is the time to build churches. Now
is the time to have revivals. Hallelujah! Now is the time to
move, now is the time to give, now is the time to pray, now
is the time to work.

It is time we hid with God and came out like firebrands
for Jesus Christ. It is time for all ministers to have a personal
revival. It is time for God's revival in the hearts of the pastors, of the evangelists, of the Bible school teachers. We
must all get in tune with God's last move. Listen, you know
what I tell my children? I say, "Children, what did your
Sunday school teacher teach you last Sunday?" They say,
"Daddy, she taught me this . . ." I want to know—I want to
know if my child's being taught by a Holy-Ghost-filled
teacher. I want to know if that teacher has the power of
God in her life or in his life. I want to know—my children's
lives are at stake.

Revivals are coming, revivals are sweeping this way. John
the Baptist is preaching. The great crowds are coming. We
are saying, "Prepare ye the way of the Lord," and one of
these hours God will pull back the curtains, the eastern skies
shall unfold, and we shall cry, "There He is! There comes
Jesus!" Oh, it will be worth everything we have ever done
for God up to that time. Every sacrifice will be paid off with
an extra reward in that glorious hour.

Now is the time to look inside your own soul to make sure
that everything is right between you and your Maker.

When my father was a young man in southern Oklahoma,
in the old Indian Territory, he said there were two families
in that community whose boy and girl fell in love with each
other. The boy would come to see her every Sunday and sit
in her parlor. Soon they were madly in love. The father
and mother of this girl became anxious because they were
not ready for their daughter to be married and they said,
"We must stop this." So the old man walked in one day and

said, "Son, you're a nice boy and all that, but we're not ready for our girl to get married and we think it's best that you don't come back." It was a pretty sad boy who walked out that day, bidding his sweetheart good-by. Time passed and the old father thought that he had stopped it but that is one way *not to stop a courtship*. This boy and girl had a mutual friend who agreed to become their go-between. This friend would take notes back and forth so that the boy kept in touch with the girl and she kept in touch with him. One day the go-between took a note from the boy's hands to the girl. She opened it. It read: "Honey, I love you. Since I've been away from you, I've just realized how much I love you." And she sent back a note telling her love for him. A little while later he sent another note and it read: "Darling, I cannot live without you." She answered, "I feel the same way." A little while later she got a note that read: "Sweetheart, will you elope with me?" She wrote right back and said she would. So there was another note that said, "On such and such a night have on your wedding clothes and be standing at your window and when you hear a gentle rap on the windowpane you'll know it will be me and I'll take you and we'll elope."

The old father got suspicious. He said, "Son, you'd better sleep in daughter's room, that fool boy might get some wild notion in his head." For several nights the boy slept in her room, but nothing happened. He said, "Oh dad, you're just dreaming things." He said, "No, you just sleep there."

The fateful day came. She went in and dressed herself in her wedding clothes and slipped an old housedress over them and finished her work. That night, she went up to her room; her brother was already fast asleep across the cot. *She* was not sleepy. She pulled her chair over by the window and sat down, waiting. All the lights were out. And you know when you are waiting for your loved one it seems like an eternity. She waited and waited. At every little sound she would stir. She would say, "He'll be here shortly." Then there would be a little sound and she would jump and say, "That's him." The hours passed away. In the wee hours of morning while she sat there doing her bravest best to keep her eyes open, she heard a little rap on the window. Her lover said, "Are you ready?" She said, "I'm ready," and she got up and slipped the old housedress off and there she was dressed in her wedding clothes. She put out her arms, he took them and lifted her out of the house and away they went. Daylight came. The old father got up and called for his daughter to cook breakfast. There was no answer. He hurried up the stairs, flung open the door, saw the boy asleep across the cot and the girl gone. He got a group of men and they combed the whole countryside, but they never found her. They found only the minister who had married them before daylight. He said, "They went thataway."

Over nineteen hundred years ago there began a courtship between Jesus and His bride. The devil killed the bridegroom and told Him not to come back. That did not stop the courtship, for we have a go-between, the blessed Holy Spirit. He is the go-between, and through the centuries and generations the Holy Spirit has been taking love notes from the bridegroom to the bride and from the bride to the bridegroom, and the love that we have for each other is ripening into maturity. Even now we are possessors of the message from God that says, "Tell the bride to expect me to come any hour."

WHAT HIS COMING WILL MEAN

The coming of the Lord Jesus will mean the *homegoing* of all the blood-washed saints of God. It means that in the twinkling of an eye, in a moment of time, tens of thousands of men and women of God shall be lifted from this earth, those who have died shall be raised from the dead and we who are living shall be translated to meet Christ in the clouds. Get this now, get this: The *missing* shall have been taken by Jesus and the *missed* will be left waiting for the appearance of antichrist. When Jesus Christ removes his people there will be nothing left to *restrain* the antichrist and the mark of the beast. The only thing that keeps antichrist away now is Christ in the saints of God who live on the earth. When they are lifted from the earth, body and soul, nothing shall be left to hold back the rise and reign of antichrist.

September of this year we lost our big tent in Amarillo, Texas, on the wind-swept plains of Texas panhandle. Winds which we believed approached a velocity of 100 miles an hour ripped the tent into a thousand pieces. I had finished my sermon and had made an altar call, and literally hundreds and hundreds of people had walked down the aisles and knelt before Christ and been saved from their sins. Then a torrential rain began falling. It came down in blinding sheets and torrents and soon the tent began to shake and the poles were picked up. We had ten men to hold each pole. I said to the great audience of 7,000 people, "You are at liberty to go—go now, but go quietly and go carefully." They did not want to go, the power of God was there. We began to sing "When the Saints Go Marching In," and all of us were in a high state of spiritual expectancy. We felt God's power and presence. I am sure that is why the people did not want to leave. There was no fear, there was no panic, we were there worshiping God. I was standing before the pulpit when the storm struck the side of the tent. I am the only man who saw the tent go up. One of our men ran out to the big trailer and turned out the lights. It was an act of God that caused him to do it. In the split second that he turned off the lights, the tent went up; there was a gust of wind that swept in out of the west and grabbed the tent and in a blinding flash of lightning I saw the tent go up as in a great volume by a gust of wind. It went up some 200 feet and settled down back over us. The big poles that held up the tent were lowered inch by inch. They were not ripped from their places and flung on the people, some invisible hand lowered them one at a time—not *on* the people but *between* the people. The big sign that weighed over 1,000 pounds just above my head that said "TURN YOUR FAITH LOOSE" was taken and blown 50 feet over my head into the audience, touching no human being. I was picked up by the wind and carried through the air and I landed on my back without a single pain. I crawled under the platform for a moment. When I saw I was all right I crawled back out, stood up and saw the huge canvas over the heads of the people. I heard people, not screaming, but singing and shouting and praising God. Two men near me looked over at me and lightning opened up the sky again and they said, "It's Brother Roberts." They said, "Brother Roberts, are you hurt?" I said, "No, I'm not hurt." One came over and put his arms around me and began to cry. "Brother Roberts, I feel the presence of Christ, don't you?"

I made my way out of the canvas and this is what happened (I'm not going to tell you all of it but I'll tell you this much of it to illustrate this message), when I got outside people saw me and of course recognized me. A man rushed up and grabbed my sleeve, he was in tears. He said, "Brother Roberts, I've lost my wife and children," he says, "I can't find them." I said, "Give me your right hand," I looked up to pray. By this time it was hailing, and beating me in the face,

I said, "God, you know where his wife and babies are, show him where to find them, for Jesus' sake." He turned and found them in less than a minute. I made my way out to the car hunting my wife and baby, I did not know where they were. I reached our car and saw it was full of people. I climbed in and a little girl was in there, she was sobbing, "I want my mommy, I want my mommy!" I poked my head out of the door, the hail hit me again, and I saw the tent lying there. People were hunting their loved ones and I said, "Oh Lord, this is like it's going to be when Jesus comes." They're going to be screaming, "Where's my boy and where's my girl? Where's my mother, where's my daddy? Where's my wife, and where's my husband? Where's my friend?" I got out of the car and spent an hour helping the people locate their loved ones.

I went all over the grounds for over an hour praying with the folks and helping them find their children. I finally found my wife and baby. I was calling them before I knew it, I was saying, "Evelyn, Evelyn, Evelyn, where are you?" About that time I met my brother Vaden and he said, "Oral, she's under the platform with Lillie Mae [his wife] and Richard Lee [that's my least little boy]." I went over there and got under the platform and said, "Evelyn, Evelyn, Evelyn!" She said, "I'm all right Oral, I'm right here." You'll never know what that meant to me. I helped her out, unhurt, unscratched. My baby didn't even have a scratch. Only 50 people received injuries; only one was serious. Only one serious injury! One man got his back broken. Seven thousand people there and one man hurt. They put him in a Catholic hospital, placed him in a cast and said he would be paralyzed for life. We prayed that God would raise him up. One week later I received a personal letter from this man. He said, "Brother Roberts, I was lying on my hospital bed in prayer, thinking about you and about the great tent, how God spared the people. I looked up and I asked Jesus to heal me and suddenly I felt my back snap in place. I pulled the cast off my body, got out of the bed and went to the sisters and said 'I'm leaving this place, I'm healed by God's power.' Oh glory to Jesus Christ of Nazareth!"

That night when we got back to our hotel the newspaper people reached us. They were exceedingly kind. The Amarillo newspapers were wonderful. Some of the reporters surveying the wreckage said, "God was here, God was here!" No man could see those ruins without saying, "God was here." God saved the people's lives. That night about one o'clock we turned on the radio and heard a special announcement: "All the people at the tent have found their loved ones. No one is missing except one little five-year-old girl. She is lost out there on the hilltop." It was hailing and the announcer was talking about the hail, and sent out an emergency call for somebody to find that child. As they closed the announcement they said this mother and father were frantic, their baby was missing. I fell on my knees and said, "God find that baby." There won't be any babies missing when Jesus comes, they are going up, neighbor. There may be dads and mothers who will not make it because they don't know God.

In a few moments the announcer said: "We are thrilled to announce the little girl has been found and re-united with her parents." I said, "Thank you, Lord."

Next morning the headlines read:

SAVING OF 7,000 CALLED
MIRACLE

Not one had been killed, fifty had received minor injuries, the one injured seriously was soon healed. Nothing I could have done in the meeting to show God's love would have demonstrated His miraculous power like the saving of the vast audience from harm and death. Over 50 were saved in the few minutes the tent was collapsing.

But the thing that lives with me is more than the intervention of God to preserve the people's lives; I was impressed by the fact that the people separated from each other found their missing loved ones.

But when Jesus appears in the clouds to "catch away his bride" millions shall be ready, millions shall not. "Two shall be in the bed the one shall be taken and the other left, two shall be grinding at the mill, the one shall be taken and the other left, two shall be in the field, the one shall be taken and the other left."

You parents are going home tonight. In a few hours the husband and the wife shall be sleeping side by side with your children asleep in another room. One is ready to meet Jesus, the other is not. Should Jesus come tonight one of you will rise, the other shall be left. Then what a weeping and wailing when the one who knows not God and is left shall awaken and find your companion gone. There will be shouting among those who have risen with Christ, but weeping among those who have not faithfully served God.

The cry will go up in every place on the earth, "Where is my wife? Where is my husband? Where are my children? Where is my father, my mother? My friends?"

It is an awful thing to be separated forever, to live such a life that you have no part with God and then find yourself *missed* when Jesus comes.

You can make sure you will be *one* who is prepared and ready for the coming of the Lord. You can know you will be one of those *missing*, not missed.

"I know that my redeemer liveth," because I am personally

acquainted with him; I know him for myself; I humbly asked him to forgive my many sins and set me free. He did it! He did it! I know my name is written there. I know my soul is right with my Saviour. I feel his holy presence tonight coursing through every fiber of my body. He thrills me, he lifts me, he blesses me.

My family is ready. My darling wife is also faithful to the Saviour, my children love Jesus. We are waiting for the Lord to come by working for God and getting men and women to hear the gospel of Bible Deliverance. Thousands and thousands of people are changing their way of living, they are humbling themselves and finding Christ. Revival victory is sweeping these dear people into the kingdom of God. More are coming in daily.

"Jesus is coming" is the urgent cry of people all over the world. "Jesus is coming" is the preaching of the full gospel ministers. "Jesus is coming" is the feeling of the true saints of God. "Jesus is coming" will soon be "Jesus has come."

"Jesus has come" will be the cry of thousands, "and I am left! Oh why didn't I listen to the message of his coming that warned me that he would soon return! Why didn't I give heed to the Scripture that said he was going to return in such an hour as I thought not!"

"Jesus has come and I am with him" will be the cry of those dear people who have their peace calling and election *sure* with God, who are living holy lives, filled with the Holy Spirit and walking in *all* the light God shines on their pathway. I intend to be in that number "when the saints go marching in."

Let every head be bowed, please.

A REED OR A ROCK—WHICH?

Scripture Text: John 1:40–42

four | A Reed or a Rock—Which?

This is Jesus' first meeting with the Big Fisherman. Andrew had met the Lord and loved Him and believed him to be the Messiah, the Christ of God. So he had gone out and found his big brother, Simon, and brought him to the Master. "Simon," he said, "this is Jesus of Nazareth, the Messiah." Simon walked up to the Lord and shook his hand. He looked into his face to see what kind of man he was. He did not realize Jesus was looking at him and was reading his life like an open book; that everything he had ever done was revealed to Jesus, and that his soul was being probed by the Son of God.

Jesus looked at Simon and knew him. He saw the worst in Simon. He saw every bad thing about him and yet loved him. Then he said, "Yes, Simon, they named you right. They certainly gave you the right name because, Simon, your name means *reed,* and that is what you are. *But thou shalt be a rock.*"

The power of love is the only power known to man that faces the worst in us and yet believes in us. Our friends know the worst about us and yet love us. Our enemies know many good things about us and yet despise us. But the Bible says that love believeth *all* things. If it were not for the love of God, every one of us would be in hell right now.

The finest thing about God is His love for lost and suffering humanity. The greatest difference between God and the devil is this one thing—love. You know, neighbor, you cannot have faith unless first, you have love. Faith is born of love. If you have no love, you cannot have faith. If you have faith, you surely have love, because it takes love to believe in someone else. It takes love to believe in God. Unless you love God, you cannot believe in Him. Unless you have a sincere reverence and worship for His holy name, you cannot say, "Lord, I believe."

If you feel like I felt when I first read this passage about Simon Peter, I am sure that you may say exactly what I said, "Sure, Jesus, you could love Simon Peter, you could have faith in *him* for he was a great man." But I changed my mind when I got behind the scenes and read this text again. Jesus looked at him and said, "There is not much to you, you big bluff fisherman, you are a coward, you have no room in your life for the cross, you would draw your sword at the drop of a hat. You meet force with force. You put your own skin above your loyalty to others. Simon, you are a *reed*."

Most of us have seen a reed. It is a fragile little thing that is blown by any wind. If the wind shifts, the reed shifts. Jesus said to Simon, "That is the kind of fellow you are."

I

But Jesus specializes in human failures. The only kind of person that God ever delivered was a failure. Think of that. The greatest successes for God in the world today were once the worst failures. The difference is God's faith in man and a person's faith in God. It is a wonderful thing that God has faith in you and me.

God looked at my poor life one day. I was a stuttering, stammering boy with tuberculosis in both lungs, a complete physical wreck. A failure. God saw me as I was and had faith that I could be changed. When *I* had faith there was a union of the faith of God in me and my faith in Him. I was set free. My tuberculosis was healed. I could talk without stuttering. I saw that I had a future.

This is God's message to all "Simons" everywhere. You may be a reed today but you shall be a rock tomorrow. This is the actual and the possible. This is today's need and tomorrow's reality. Today's want and tomorrow's realization.

The buddies and neighbors of Simon said, "Jesus, it can't be done. We know Simon; we've fished with him; we've gambled with him; we've fought with him; we've drunk liquor with him; we've traveled with him; we've carried on business with him; we know him. Oh, he's got a big heart, he's a wonderful fellow in a way but talk about Simon being a *rock*—you don't know much about him, do you?"

His neighbors said, "Not Simon, you'll not change *him* into a rock. We live next door to him. We know how he makes new resolutions every year that he is going to be a different man and we know how he breaks every resolution, too, before the year is out. Yes, we know Simon, Jesus, and you are not going to make him into a rock."

Jesus smiled and said, "Yes, he will be a rock."

The difference between people and God is that people are used to human wrecks and nothing being done about changing them. God has faith that human wrecks can be changed through His love and faith and power. Jesus agreed with them that Simon could not be changed if he continued living as he was, neither could he be changed through his own strength or power. Jesus was counting on something else—

faith in God. He knew that what no man can do, faith in God can do.

Jesus said, "Thou art Simon, a reed."

II

Who is Simon? What did Jesus mean when he called Simon a reed?

1. Simon was a man who by his own admission was a sinful man. One day Simon was mending his broken nets, he and his buddies. Their ship was anchored nearby. Jesus said, "Whose boat is that?"

Someone answered, "It is Simon's."

He found Simon and said, "Simon, will you lend me your boat for the preaching of the gospel?"

Simon replied, "Sure, Master, help yourself."

Jesus said, "Simon, shove the boat out a ways from the shore."

He did. Jesus climbed into the boat and preached his message of hope and faith. He preached until the raging torment in men's bosom was stilled. He preached until their fear had quietened. He preached until their faith had reached up and touched the hem of his garment. He preached until women dried their tears and men hushed their voices. He preached until little children sat enraptured and transfixed in his divine presence and when he got through, he turned to Simon and said, "Simon, I thank you for lending me your boat. Now get in here with me and launch out into the deep and let down your net for a catch of fish."

"Jesus," Simon said, "that was a powerful sermon you preached today. I've never heard anything like it, but I see right now you don't know much about fishing, do you? Take me, for instance, I was raised on the blue waters of Galilee.

I am a commercial fisherman. I know these waters like you know your own backyard, and listen, we have toiled all night and haven't even caught one fish!"

I think I know how he felt. He had made a water-haul. About the most discouraged human being I ever saw was a fellow who fished all day or all night and never got a bite.

And he said, "Lord, you just don't know what you are talking about. You had better stick to preaching and leave the fishing to me."

Jesus said, "Simon, you cannot do anything for God without receiving something in return. Now get in this boat and launch out in the deep."

Simon said, "Lord, I don't think we'll catch anything but, nevertheless, at thy word, I will do it."

Jesus teaches the principle of *reciprocity:* you cannot give something to God without receiving something better in return. You cannot be a tither without having those tithes multiplied and returned to you. You cannot contribute money to the work of Christ without having that money restored to you many times. You cannot give your talents to Christ without those talents further enriching your life.

So Simon launched forth. They got away out there in deep water and Jesus said, "Right here, throw your net over on the right side." And in a few moments they had caught a net-breaking, boat-sinking load of fish. Jesus knew where the fish were. He is the *master fisherman* of life. Simon threw his net over the side in obedience to Jesus and he caught more fish than he could handle. The Bible says his "net brake." He had to call his partners over. He cried, "Come over and help us."

Neighbor, when you give something to God and He climbs into your fishing boat and goes fishing at your side, you are going to catch a net-breaking, boat-sinking load of Bible deliverance, of peace and happiness and the joy of Jesus Christ of Nazareth.

A couple of years ago, I went fishing with Lee Braxton at Lake Waccamaw in North Carolina. Mrs. Roberts and I got a little boat and Lee hired us a colored guide. An old man who knew those waters for forty years. Lee said, "Brother Roberts, you do just exactly what this old guide says and I guarantee you will catch fish." Well, I didn't know exactly what Lee had in mind. I didn't find out until we were about a mile from the shore. This fellow directed us to anchor the boat and bait our hooks. We did. Then he did one of the strangest things I ever saw. He leaned over the side of the boat and began to beat the side with his right hand.

I said, "Say, fellow, you will scare all the fish in the lake away."

He said, "Reverend, I have been fishing in these waters forty years. At this time of the year if you will beat the side of the boat you will catch perch. Now while I beat the side of the boat, throw out your line and you will catch fish."

I said, "Mister, just beat the side of this boat all you want to."

While he beat the sides of the boat we began catching fish. We caught them practically as fast as we could get them off the hook. When we got through, I shook his hand, gave him an extra tip and told him I wanted to go fishing with him again. That old man knew how to catch fish. We caught enough fish for a big fish-fry that evening.

Jesus Christ knows exactly how to direct men to success, to prosper and to receive the things in life they want most.

All the way back to the shore, Simon looked at those big fish, then he would look at the Lord. When he got to the shore, he pulled the net of fish out on the dry land. Then he looked at his hands and as he did he thought of his life: how whipped and defeated he was through his own sins; how strong habits of sin controlled his every thought: how bound and frustrated he was. Without another word he just pitched over in the sand with tears streaming down his face. Jesus walked over and said, "Simon! Simon!" He looked up and said, "Depart from me, Lord, for I am a sinful man."

He did not realize that he had not conquered sin until he had come into the white light of the presence of Jesus Christ. He had seen the outstretched arm of the Lord catch fish after he and his crew had toiled all night and caught nothing. Now he realized all that he had been missing and all that was lacking in his life.

He was a man who was raised up in the most orthodox manner. He had been reared in the church and had gone to the sabbath schools in the synagogue. He had heard the word of God and was a church member in good standing yet he had not won the victory over sin. This is the picture of thousands of religious people around the world. They have never won the victory over sin nor conquered their evil habits.

Neighbor, you can win the victory over sin if you want that victory. It is a terrible doctrine that teaches that men through faith cannot conquer sin. How wicked it is when men preach that you cannot live a holy life. Paul said, "Without holiness no man shall see the Lord." There is victory in Jesus Christ to every person who wants to conquer the power of sin. Thousands are winning this victory through faith in God. It is victory Jesus promises to all people everywhere.

2. *And then Simon had no room for the cross in his life.* Jesus said to his disciples, "I must needs suffer. I must go to Jerusalem where I will be tried by the Chief Priests and the Elders and I shall be crucified and I shall go to the cross." The Bible says that Simon, "took him and rebuked him."

Now the word "took" is so strong that we believe Simon *shook* Jesus like he would shake a naughty child.

"Lord," he said, "this shall not be so unto thee."

Jesus said, "Get thee behind me, Satan, for thou savourest not the things that be of God but the things that be of men. Except a man shall take up his own cross and follow me, he is none of mine; for if a man shall save his life he shall lose it and if a man shall lose his life for my sake he shall find it again."

Simon had no room for the cross of Christ.

Jesus stated further, "But if a man shall save his own life he shall lose it and if a man shall lose his life for my sake, he shall find it." That is a paradox. Jesus is saying, "If you cling to your own identity, if you take life into your own hands and fight your battles then you will lose your identity. You will be a nameless blot on the pages of eternity." On the other hand, he says, "If you will lose your life for my sake, you will find it." That means, if you let the life of Christ flow through your life, if you merge your identity and name with his, you will *save* your life because only what you do for God and right will survive.

I am not interested in taking life into my own incapable hands. Frankly, I do not know how to run my life or to fight my battles. Every time I have tried I have lost. I have found myself frustrated and tormented by inner conflicts and fears. But every time I have lost my way by taking the way of Jesus I have won.

If you take the cross of Jesus Christ from my life I remain a tubercular patient, a stuttering, stammering boy. The cross means everything to me. I stake my very soul on the cross of Calvary. I know from whence my power cometh—from the name of Jesus Christ of Nazareth.

A few months ago, my dear, sweet mother, a spirit-filled

saint of God, said to me, "Oral, don't ever forget that once you had t.b., that once you stammered and stuttered and could not talk. You owe everything to what God has done for you."

I said, "You are right, mama, and thank you for reminding me. I don't ever want to turn my back on the Saviour who gave me the power of God."

My wife says to me, "Oral, keep humble in the sight of God. What you have is His power. It is not yours, it is His. Keep humble and you will always have God's presence and power."

3. *Next, Simon had a "gimme" spirit.* One day a rich young ruler who came to Christ said, "Lord, what must I do to have this wonderful life that you are speaking about. I have many *possessions,* I have kept the commandments but I don't have this life that you are describing." The Bible says that Jesus, looking on him, "loved him." He said, "Young man, sell what you have and give; come follow me and thou shalt have *treasures.*"

The young man turned away sorrowfully for he had great possessions. Notice the difference Jesus made between treasures and possessions. He said, "Sell your *possessions* and give to the poor; follow me and I will give you *treasures.*" Jesus said there is a vast difference between treasures and possessions. Possessions are tangible things such as houses, lands, clothes, automobiles and money. These are possessions. But Jesus says, "Come follow me and I will give you treasures." Jesus means there is a treasure far greater than the possessions of the rich young ruler. He did not have this treasure. The young man walked away sorrowfully because he had only "great possessions."

Simon Peter turned to Jesus and said, "Look, Lord, we've forsaken all, we've given up our fishing nets, we've left our fathers and mothers. What shall we have therefore. What are we going to get out of it?"

Jesus said, "Simon, everybody who has forsaken houses and lands or mothers or fathers or brothers or sisters or wives or children for my sake shall have a hundredfold and life-everlasting." In other words, *a hundredfold of life itself.* Jesus meant that life itself is a treasure but to those who follow him he will give a *hundredfold* of life.

Let me explain further. This young man had possessions. He realized they were not satisfying him. Jesus offered him an equal trade. The treasures of an enriching, satisfying, abundant life. Peace of soul, peace of mind, faith. These things the young man did not have. He clung to his possessions and gave up the treasures.

Simon said, "All right, what are *we* going to get."

Jesus reminded him of the treasures he already had. A hundredfold of life itself.

When we were in Minneapolis, Minnesota, in one of our meetings there, a deacon from the Baptist church came in the healing line. He was crippled with arthritis. He said, "Brother Roberts, I have just been dismissed from Mayo clinic. I stayed there four months. I paid them 12,000 cash dollars for them to cure my body only to hear them say, 'We have done all we can; we cannot hold out hope for a cure whatever. You can go home.' I have returned home a cripple having paid $12,000 to be cured." That is what he told me. What could *I* offer him? I could not promise him possessions but I could, through Jesus' power in me, offer him the things money cannot buy and there is a great difference between things that money can buy and things that money cannot buy. I thank God tonight because there are some things that money cannot secure. If it took money, only the rich folks would have God. The poor never would have a chance. I never would have had an opportunity to have been saved or healed for I have known deepest poverty.

I said to this man, "Sir, we don't want your money. Forget about your money and in a moment's time you can have what money cannot buy. You can receive healing in the name of Jesus Christ of Nazareth." I laid my right hand upon this man and in earnest believing prayer, I asked Jesus Christ to have mercy upon him and heal his body. I stood there and watched his legs straighten out. I saw his right arm come loose. I saw him leap off the platform with his body healed. As he ran down the aisle perfectly whole, I thought of the $12,000 he had just paid to get a cure which they said was beyond the reach of human power, yet Jesus Christ gave him the treasure which he had lost. The treasure of a sound body. I am sure he did not worry about the money he gave the doctors to get well. With this new treasure he would earn more money.

When I think of the $12,000 that he paid only to be sent home a hopeless case, I am made to realize that without a single penny, he received perfect healing and deliverance in a moment's time. When I think of that, I can tell you there is a vast difference between treasures and possessions.

You know, neighbor, money is the cheapest thing in the world. It is getting cheaper every day. It is buying less and less of less and less. If Jesus Christ promised men money, he would be stooping beneath their actual need because money is such a futile little thing when it comes to getting the things that count most in life. You cannot buy peace for a human soul. You cannot buy peace of mind. You cannot buy health. You cannot buy happiness. You cannot buy friendship or love. You cannot make a baby love you because a baby either loves you or he does not. Babies love people who love them. They cannot be deceived. A baby knows if you love it. That is one way to know if your minister has love. If the children love your minister, he is usually a good man. If you will watch your children, they will help you in securing the right kind of preacher. Money cannot buy that kind of love.

Money cannot even buy a good night's sleep. They make sleeping pills in this day for people who cannot sleep. Many of them take the pills and never wake up until they get into another world. Yet there is an infallible secret of success for every human being to do the thing that he ought to do to be happy. When I said that God does not promise money, I meant to say that God promises all the things money cannot buy. God promises you all the money you need *plus* all the things that money cannot buy.

When Simon asked, "What am I going to get out of it?" Jesus answered, "This is what you are going to get. In this world you will have fathers and mothers; you will have treasures; you will have your needs supplied according to my riches in glory; you will have everything in life that counts." God is so rich he hangs up solid pearls for his gates and paves the streets with whole slabs of pure gold. The walls are solid jasper and the foundation is garnished with all manner of precious stones. Some of you women here are wearing huge diamonds that almost knock my eyes out as I stand up here and preach. Some of those stones are five and ten carat diamonds. That is nothing, lady, that is nothing. Why, the foundation of God's holy city has stones of such size that they *support* the entire city. God is not poor. God is rich, and every bit of it is ours *plus all the things that money cannot buy*.

A woman who came in the healing line in our meeting in Memphis, Tennessee, was wearing the largest diamond I had ever seen. I seldom ever notice people's diamonds but this one was so huge and had such a flash until I could not miss seeing it. I said to her, "Lady, if I needed that diamond to use in the support of my ministry, what would you do?"

She pulled it off and said, "Here."

I said, "No, take it back, take it back. I just wanted to know if you had that kind of spirit." People, you will find that those who really love God have everything they possess available for the services of Jesus Christ. Every possession is at God's disposal. To such people "treasures" mean more than "possessions."

Jesus teaches us that we are to tithe our money to his service and have all the rest on reserve for the Lord to tap at any time that he needs it.

4. *Then Simon unsheathed his sword when he faced the battles of life.* He met force with force. Jesus was arrested while in prayer. Judas Iscariot betrayed him with a kiss; they laid rough and rude hands upon him and led him away to be tried. Simon jerked out his sword and whacked off the ear of the high priest's servant. Jesus healed and restored the man's ear and sharply rebuked Simon, saying, "Simon, put up thy sword for they that live by the sword shall perish by the sword." Simon put up his sword and Jesus was crucified. The world scoffs and says, "What a philosophy." The world cannot understand this. It is almighty meekness versus human force. Which is the stronger? Almighty meekness or human force? The conquered or the conqueror? The slain or the victor? Who won that day when Jesus submitted to force while they slapped his cheeks and spit in his face and sent him to the cross? Who won that day? Unquestionably, almighty meekness won.

Jesus said, "If you live by the sword, you will perish by the sword." This means if you meet force by force you will perish by force. If you take your life into your own incapable hands then by the weakness of your hands you will be destroyed. If you are one of those people who is always flying off the handle and fighting somebody with your fists you are going to meet someone whose fists are harder than yours and he will "knock your block off." If you are one of those people who has a long tongue that is always whittling on somebody's reputation, and going across this great city and whacking at someone's influence and character—if you use your tongue as your defense, then somebody is going to have a sharper tongue than you and with it they will cut you down.

This is the master principle by which Jesus Christ operates: almighty meekness rather than human force.

Well, somebody says, "Simon put up his sword and they crucified Jesus." That is right *but,*

> "Truth crushed to earth will rise again
> The eternal years of God are hers.
> But error wounded, writhes in pain,
> And lies amid her worshippers."

Crushed truth has in it the seeds of resurrection. They bruised him, they humiliated him, they killed him, they buried him and left him in the tomb; but when they buried Jesus they buried *crushed truth.* The third day he rose from the dead, alive forevermore.

You can afford to be beaten down today if you know you will rise tomorrow. You can afford to be hounded and humiliated and criticized today if you know you will be unconquerable when the sun rises in the morning. And yet many of us are fighting our own battles and losing every one of them. We are fretting, worrying, and tormented by our own fear. All because we are not submitting our way to God so that he can fight our battles. "If God be for us who can be against us?"

Jesus said, "Put up thy sword." Personally, I can say I have got over fighting force by force because I have lost too many battles. The only victories I have ever won have been through meekness. Meekness is not *weakness*. Meekness is *power* because meekness is based on faith, not fear. Men use force because they are afraid. They use force, not because they feel superior, but because they believe they are inferior. They are afraid they are going to lose. Meekness enables a man to submit his cause to Jesus Christ believing he is superior to every outside circumstance and condition and that God, who has never lost a battle, will take his cause and plead it successfully. Meekness is putting your cause in the hands of a higher power so that it is God's cause, not yours.

5. *Simon put his own safety above his loyalties.* When Simon got into a tight place where his testimony would be tried he was thinking of his own hide rather than his loyalty to the Saviour.

While Jesus was being tried for his life, Simon walked into Pilate's Hall and at the door someone said, "Say, you look like one of the disciples of Jesus." He said, "Get out of my way, I don't even know the man." He saw a group of men standing around a charcoal fire. He went over there to warm. But Jesus wasn't worrying about fire. Simon went to the fire because he felt the cold. How did he know it was cold? Because he was in the wrong place at the wrong time. One night I was preaching and I got so inspired in my spirit that I struck the pulpit with the knuckles of my hand and it brought the blood and cut a gash in my hand. I did not know I had done it until I got to my room. Later, I was washing my hands and saw that I had a gash in my hand. I said to myself, "I wonder where I got that?" It didn't hurt. *I had been so lost in my message that I did not know I had hurt myself.* Neighbor, you won't notice the cold and heat when you serve God like other people notice cold and heat. You do not stay away from God's house just because it is raining or snowing. Folks who whine about the weather and about their little troubles are putting their own skin above their loyalties. Simon was warming his hands when a little maid walked up and said, "Say, you talk like one of those Nazarenes."

He replied, "I don't even know what you are talking about."

Pretty soon, someone else walked up and stated, "Your speech betrays you."

Simon said, "I'll show you I am not one of them," and he began to curse.

That is one way to prove that you do not belong to Jesus. When you curse, it is a testimony that you do not belong to the Almighty God. I know many church people who curse. They wonder why they curse. Because they have not the tender, meek spirit of Jesus. Men whose souls are clean do not have filthy tongues. When you curse you show the kind of heart you have.

This is Simon the Reed, Jesus said, "Thou art Simon."

III

He also said, "Thou shalt be Peter, the Rock."

I have seen myself in Simon, haven't you? I have seen myself walking down the old road where the reed is blown by every wind. But that is not all the story. Jesus said, "Thou shalt be," and "Thou shalt be" he was. What does all this mean?

It means that Simon was capable of *being saved* and *worth saving.* I appreciate that. For Jesus Christ looks into the face of every human being and says, "You are worth changing. You are worth saving. You are capable of being changed by my power."

IV

Peter became a rock. How?

First of all, through divine providence. What is providence? Providence is the watchful care and intervention of a loving God unseen and unsolicited on our part. It is the intervening of the mighty hand of God unseen. He works in mysterious ways His wonders to perform.

Here is what happened. There were many exits to the Hall of Pilate but do you know the one that Jesus took? The one near where Simon was standing with his broken testimony. Simon was standing where Jesus could give him *that look*. It was the look of Jesus that saved Simon's life, changing his whole career so that he was transformed from a rood to the granite structure of the rock itself. Simon could have been standing in any other place in the Hall of Pilate and yet he was standing exactly where Christ would pass by him. Isn't that wonderful?

When Jesus walked through the Hall of Pilate on his way to the cross, he saw Simon Peter and stopped. Luke says that he "looked" on Simon.

Somebody said that he gave Simon a look of wounded love. I have never seen wounded love in the look of Jesus. Simon was a man—a rough man—and I seriously doubt if a look of wounded love would have sent him out to weep. You do not make men weep by looking sorrowfully at them. You cannot appeal to a broad shouldered, deep chested hunk of a man like Simon by looking at him with wounded eyes.

What kind of look did Jesus give Simon? There was *some-*

thing in the face of Jesus that caused Simon Peter to go out and weep his way back to God. I will tell you what it was: it was the *same look* that Jesus had given him three years before when he met him the first time. The face of Jesus said, (and remember Jesus himself didn't say a word, he just looked at Simon) "Yes, thou art Simon, a reed." Simon began to back off and say, "Yes, that's what I am. I've denied you three times. I've been untrue, unfaithful," and as he backed off slowly, the face of Jesus changed. And his look said, "But thou shalt be Peter the Rock."

Simon stopped and said, "You mean that I can still become Peter the Rock?"

Jesus nodded and walked on. When Simon realized that Jesus Christ had faith in him, it broke him to pieces. He hurried outside the Hall of Pilate, put his face up against the wall and cried like a whipped child. The Bible says he "wept bitterly." Through the look of *faith* on Jesus' face Simon saw the light of God and found his way back.

2. *The morning Jesus rose from the dead, the angel from heaven said to Mary, "Jesus said to go and tell his disciples and Peter that he will meet them in Galilee."* And Peter! And so Mary ran up and pounded on the door, "Disciples! Peter! Open the door." They opened the door and she said, "Listen! Listen! Jesus has sent the angel to me and the angel said for me to tell you, especially you, Peter, that he is going to meet you all in Galilee."

Men and women, God told me to tell you that He was going to see you. He is going to reveal himself to you in some way.

3. *So they went to Galilee.* One frosty morning they were out on the blue waters of Galilee fishing. A stranger walked upon the shore. He saw them out there. Cupping his hands to his mouth, he said, "Children! Children! Have you any

meat?" Somebody on the boat said, "There is a stranger on the shore calling to us." Again they heard his voice, "Children! Children! Have you any meat?" John said, "It is the Lord!"

Simon jumped out of the boat and raced toward the shore. When they arrived, Jesus had prepared a meal for them and he said, "Come and dine." He has been saying that ever since.

When they got through eating the fish and honeycomb, Jesus looked at the bones of the fish scattered near the fire and said, "Simon, lovest thou me more than these?"

"Yea, Lord."

"Feed my lambs."

"Simon, lovest thou me more than these?"

"Yea, Lord."

"Feed my sheep."

"Simon, lovest thou me more than these?"

"Yea, Lord, you know I love you."

He said, "Yes, I know. Feed my sheep."

4. He saw that Simon really loved Him. He saw something else, too. He saw the reed fade and disappear and in its place the outline of granite rock. He said, "Go to the upper room and tarry until ye be endued with power from on high. Ye shall be baptized with the Holy Ghost and with fire not many days hence."

They went to the upper room with Peter in the lead. The rock now is beginning to take shape. Pentecost morning came. There was no further dissension among the disciples, no bickering for when the day of Pentecost was fully come they were all in one accord. They were sweetly sanctified long before Pentecost morning dawned for they had *oneness of spirit*. Likemindedness. Nobody felt above anyone else. That is the kind of folks who receive the Holy

Spirit and that is exactly why more people are not receiving the Holy Ghost. It takes the deepest unselfishness to bring one into the attitude where he can be filled with the Holy Ghost and fire.

So on Pentecost morning, they were so unified that they were like pieces of steel inseparably welded together. All of a sudden there was a heavenly sound which filled the house where they were sitting and they were all filled with the Holy Ghost and began to speak with other tongues as the Holy Spirit gave their lips utterance.

When they got through speaking and magnifying God, Peter said to the eleven, "Follow me." They went out on the streets, raised their voices in testimony, and preached the name of Jesus Christ of Nazareth. It was Peter who gave the altar call. It was the "Rock" that raised up his hand and said, "Flee the wrath to come." Three thousand men and women followed his advice—the advice of the man who became a rock through the power of Jesus Christ.

5. *They put the "Rock" in jail and in his deliverance you will find one of the finest things about the Lord's power.* Simon was secured between two soldiers in the innermost part of the prison. There he lay asleep one night when an angel tapped him on the shoulder and said, "Peter, rise and follow me." He opened his eyes and thought it was a dream but the angel standing before him was not a vision. When Peter saw that he was neither asleep nor seeing a vision, he jumped up and found that his chains had fallen off. The angel said, "Follow me." When they got to the first gate, the angel pulled out a set of keys and turned one of them in the lock. Likewise on the second gate. *God's angel has a key to every human lock.* When they got to the big gate that opened toward the city and the gate saw the angel and the *Rock* coming, it opened up on its own accord.

SHADOW OF PETER

6. Even the shadow *of Peter the Rock brought healing to the sick and afflicted.* His ministry of healing became so popular that multitudes of people poured into Jerusalem from every part of the land.

Soon Peter found there was no way to minister to them. He was not able to pray for them separately.

Someone conceived the idea of having all these sick people line the streets so that when the great apostle came near enough for his shadow to fall upon them they should use his shadow as their *point of contact.* The Bible states, "Insomuch that they brought the sick into the streets, and laid them on beds and couches, that at the least the shadow of Peter passing by might overshadow some of them . . . and they were healed everyone."

What a wonderful thing this is. God used the *shadow* of the man changed from reed to rock. What power our Lord has.

And why was Peter called Rock. Because he had become a piece of *that rock* Jesus Christ. And here is the significance. No door, no chain, no force can imprison the man who has been changed through his faith in the Son of God. When your faith in Jesus Christ brings his power to bear upon your life and you are changed from a reed into a rock there will be no door that shall close in your face, no chain that can bind your life. The doors will swing open and you will pass through to victory. Changed. Made over again and you wouldn't trade back for ten thousand worlds like this. Do you believe it? Let every head be bowed, please.

DEMON POSSESSION

five | Demon Possession

Turn with me to the book of Matthew, chapter 12, verse 43—Jesus said, "When the unclean spirit is gone out of a man, he walketh through dry places, seeking rest, and findeth none." He does not mean the man walks through dry places, He means that the demon spirits that come out of him walk through dry places, seeking rest, and findeth none. "Then he saith, I will return into my house from whence I came out; and when he is come, he findeth it empty, swept, and garnished. Then goeth he, and taketh with himself seven other spirits more wicked than himself, and they enter in and dwell there; and the last state of that man is worse than the first. Even so shall it be also unto this wicked generation."

Now in the 5th chapter of Mark, beginning at verse 1: "And they came over unto the other side of the sea, into the country of the Gadarenes. And when he was come out of the ship, immediately there met him out of the tombs a man with an unclean spirit, Who had his dwelling among the tombs; and no man could bind him, no, not with chains: Because that he had been often bound with fetters and chains, and the chains had been plucked asunder by him, and the fetters broken in pieces; neither could any man tame him.

109

And always, night and day, he was in the mountains, and in the tombs, crying, and cutting himself with stones. But when he saw Jesus afar off, he ran and worshipped him, And cried with a loud voice, and said, What have I to do with thee, Jesus, thou Son of the most high God? I adjure thee by God, that thou torment me not. For he said unto him, Come out of the man, thou unclean spirit. And he asked him, What is thy name? And he answered, saying, My name is Legion: for we are many. And he besought him much that he would not send them away out of the country. Now there was there nigh unto the mountains a great herd of swine feeding. And all the devils besought him, saying, Send us into the swine, that we may enter into them. And forthwith Jesus give them leave. And the unclean spirits went out, and entered into the swine; and the herd ran violently down a steep place into the sea (they were about two thousand) and were choked in the sea."

There were 2,000 hogs that perished—we know at least there were 2,000 demons in this one man. At least 2,000!

"And they that fed the swine fled, and told it in the city, and in the country. And they went out to see what it was that was done. And they come to Jesus, and see him that was possessed with the devil, and had the legion, sitting, and clothed, and in his right mind: and they were afraid."

This world has always been afraid of people in their right minds.

"And they that saw it told them how it befell to him that was possessed with the devil, and also concerning the swine. And they began to pray him to depart out of their coasts."

This world has always had room for demons but none for God.

"And when he was come into the ship, he that had been possessed with the devil prayed him that he might be with him. Howbeit Jesus suffered him not, but saith unto him, Go home to thy friends, and tell them how great things the Lord hath done for thee, and hath had compassion on thee. And he departed, and began to publish in Decapolis how great things Jesus had done for him: and all men did marvel."

Now in Ephesians, chapter 6, are some of the most significant statements in the entire Bible concerning demons. Beginning at verse 10, Paul said, "Finally, my brethren, be strong in the Lord, and in the power of his might. Put on the whole armour of God, that ye may be able to stand against the wiles of the devil. For we wrestle not against flesh and blood, but against principalities, against powers, against the rulers of the darkness of this world, against spiritual wickedness (or rulers) in high places. Wherefore take unto you the whole armour of God, that ye may be able to withstand in the evil day (that's our day), and having done all, to stand. *Stand therefore . . . .*"

The psychologists say that these two words, "Stand therefore," form the most powerful statement that a man can utter when he is in a time of stress or conflict. Stand therefore!

Now as I bring this message on demon possession, I want everybody to relax. I am going to quit when I get through, but I'm not going to quit until I do get through. I have something to say. God has given me a ministry against demons, so if you have ever been reverent in your life be reverent while I preach the word of God to you about demons tonight.

MY FEAR OF DEMONS

All my life I have been afraid of demons. My oldest sister was tormented by these strange powers. From the age of five until she was nineteen she had convulsions. When she was nineteen, God, in mercy, took her soul to a better world than this. Friday night in my life story from this platform I'll tell you about what happened to my sister and the mark made on me when I was a little child crawling on the ground in the front yard of our home, out in the country, in Oklahoma.

My father has been a minister all my life. He is a minister now, and he has always warned me against demons. He said, "Oral, when you come to cast out demons, unless you have the power of God over demons you're in great danger of being attacked yourself." Prior to my special call from God in May, 1947, I was called upon to cast out demon spirits only a few times. Each time I faced people possessed with demons, I had a great fear and trembling. I was fearful that they would attack me. Therefore, I never had much success in casting out demons. But when Jesus spoke to me in an audible voice and said, "From this hour you will heal the sick and cast out demons by my power," I believed his word unto me; the awful fear was lifted from me like you take a wet blanket off somebody. I was able to face the demons in those people possessed with them, with no fear whatever but with great faith in God and power in my life. I shall never forget the first experience I had shortly afterward. I had a long healing line facing me in Oklahoma. A woman came before me who was possessed with many demons. When I started to pray for her the demons violently seized her body and threw her on the ground at my feet. Her head struck the floor and it seemed that it would pop open. She lay there writhing and kicking and gnawing her tongue, foaming at the mouth, her hands turned in toward her body. I did not know what to do, I had never seen anyone cast out demons and had no successful experience myself up till that time. I faced her, not knowing where to turn; suddenly the spirit of God came upon me and I trembled with God's presence. I reached down, took her hand in my right hand and said, "Thou foul tormenting demons, I adjure thee in the Name of Jesus Christ of Nazareth, come out of this woman! Loose her and let her go free!" Instantly her body shook from head to toe; she raised up her head and looked at me. I did not know what was going to happen. I did not even know that she was healed because I had had no previous experience. When the Lord's power came upon me I took His command over the demons. Suddenly she looked up at me. I saw her countenance change. I said, "In Jesus' name, rise!" She sprang to her feet like some invisible force had lifted her, threw up her hands and began crying, "Jesus Christ has healed me and has made me free!" That was my first time to cast out demons through God's power and I won the victory in Jesus' name over the first demons I faced!

From that time there has been ever-increasing power in my life to cast out demons. Each miracle of healing wrought by God through my faith has given me strength and courage. A few months later, I was praying for a deaf child. I had never faced deaf spirits or at least none that I knew about. I was having no success with this child and suddenly God spoke to me. It was the third time that I ever heard Him in an audible voice. He said, "My servant, you have been faithful. Now you shall feel my power in your right hand. You shall detect the presence of demons and know their number and name and will have my power to cast them out."

Immediately that power came in my right hand. I felt a strange and glorious sensation like an electrical current flowing through my hand. It was God's healing power. I discerned and detected the deaf spirits in this child and brought immediate and complete healing to him in a moment's time, gave him back to his mother and from that time that strange power that God said I would have has worked in my hand. I cannot explain it to anybody, it simply is there when God says it will be there and through that power I detect the presence of demons and cast them out of suffering humanity.

RECOGNIZING DEMONS

Many times I know there are demon-possessed people in the audience before anybody else ever knows. Many times I know they are in the healing line before they ever get to me, because I can feel them through God's power of discernment in me. When I lay my hand upon their head or I take their hand in my right hand and the spirit of God comes in my hand, then I feel this sensation in my hand. Demons have power too. Their power is challenged by God's power in my hand. I discern them by name and number just like you take the pages of a book and count the pages as you turn them one by one. Pressure of the demons comes against God's power in my hand like that and I count the number of the demons by the strange pressure they make. I count them— one, two, three, four, five, six or seven and I know exactly how many demons are there and their names. God gives me their names so that I know what kind each demon is. As I pray the strong pressure of the demons comes against me, like a strong man is pushing me back. Then as God's power comes in my hand against the demon-pressure the demons give way. God's power increases until there is nothing left reacting against His presence in me. A great joy wells up within me and pretty soon I am shouting, "There they go! There they go!" And they are cast out by the power of Jesus Christ, the Son of God!

This is one of the signs that Jesus is coming soon and that we are in the last days. The nearer we get to the end-time— these preachers will tell you this—the nearer we get to the Lord's coming the more demons are going to work, and possess people and torment them; and the more God is going to give His servants power to cast them out. "For where sin doth abound, grace doth much more abound!"

THE POWER OF DEMONS

The power of demons is simply appalling. I never knew the frightful power of demons until God revealed Himself to me concerning my present ministry. Of course, I heard them whisper that my sister had demons. All my life I have heard Papa and Mama talk of how Velma was afflicted. I remember seeing Velma only a few times since I was only a child when she died. But during the brief years I have been in this ministry I have begun to realize the awesome power of demon spirits. I know the Bible teaches their power and I have seen that power with my own eyes. I have brought God's deliverance to thousands of the demon-possessed. Those who have *unclean demons* have what I call, "snake eyes." Their eyes look exactly like the eyes of a serpent. I am not talking about those who have epileptic spirits or who have a deaf and dumb spirit or a spirit of fear. I am not talking about that. I refer only to the unclean demons referred to in the Bible. When they seize a person, he becomes exactly what the demon is; the demons take complete control and look from their eyes and speak with their tongue and use their mind, soul and body. Demons have personalities. They are *evil* spirits. They are as much a personality as a human being is a personality. They can speak and their language is intelligible one to the other in their own special way, but they can speak as a human speaks by using the tongue of a human being.

The Bible speaks of their power in the story about the man who had at least 2,000 unclean demons in him (there were 2,000 hogs and when the demons came out of him they went in those hogs, who in turn perished in the sea. This man's name was legion which means an indefinable number; it *could* mean a thousand or two thousand or even fifty thousand) and when they chained him he would break those chains as though they were twine strings. No man could tame him and he lived among the graves and the tombs day and night, cutting himself, crying and living in torment. He was possessed of unclean demons.

The Bible speaks of a young woman who was possessed of many demons, the spirits of divination (fortune-telling demons in our own everyday language) or familiar demons, so that she became psychic in her personality. Men used this girl, making merchandise of her satanic talent. People came in such large numbers to have her tell them their fortunes, that her masters were waxing rich through this infamous traffic in human life.

Paul and Silas came into town preaching a mighty revival with signs and wonders and this young girl saw them and began to follow them. Demons know God, they know Jesus and they know the servants of Jesus; the demons used her voice, saying, "Paul, Silas! Thou servants of the most High God, we know thee who thou art." Day after day she followed them and these demons screamed out their names and that they were the servants of the most High God. Paul's spirit was stirred within him and he turned one day and said to these demons, "I adjure thee by Jesus, come out of her and enter no more into her!" The demons came out of her, she was free; she could not tell fortunes any more and her owners who possessed her, body and soul, were mad and infuriated at Paul and Silas and had them thrown into jail.

This world loves sin. This world loves the demon-world. This world does not care about the work of Bible Deliverance.

What does the world care about healing of the sick or the casting out of demon spirits? We are in an unfriendly, cold, wicked world tonight! There are thousands of people who are losing their souls. They are turning from God and going to fortune-tellers, all of whom having real psychic powers are possessed with demon spirits. They have turned away from the knowledge of the Lord God. God can tell a man or woman more in five minutes than he or she would ever learn in a lifetime by dealing with demon-possessed people; but people love sin; they love darkness. *There is a curse upon such people: the curse of God is upon every man and woman who turns to someone with a familiar spirit.* Unless you repent and get right with God you will go straight to hell!

These are the last days and anything you have been doing outside the will of God—stop it now! If you want the peace of God in this world and in the world to come, make a break with anything that would destroy your soul.

Paul conducted a great revival of God's power at Ephesus. People came out to hear and see the miracles he performed through Jesus Christ. There were such tremendous miracles in that revival until the people who dealt in "black magic and witchcraft" burned their *curious* books.

There was a vagabond Jew, an exorcist—similar to a spiritualist medium today—who had seven sons who watched Paul cast out demons through the name of Jesus. These young exorcists found a demon-possessed man, gathered around him, and said to the demons, "We adjure thee by Jesus Whom Paul preaches, come out of this man," and the demons using the tongue of this demon-possessed man said, "Paul we know, Jesus we know but who are you?" The demons gave the man they possessed such strength that he leaped upon the seven men, tore their clothes off, wounded them and threw them out of the house in the street. Great fear fell upon the people in Ephesus and they gave glory to God because of this display of the power of Jesus Christ against demons. But imagine, if you can, the tremendous power the demons exercised through their victim against the seven sons of Sceva.

MEN SHOULD BE REVERENT

I have seen the demons twist people's bodies. One night I was praying for people in the healing line. Several were present to be delivered from demons. I always ask people to be reverent, to remain seated with heads bowed. A man over on my right would not bow his head, he was making fun and sitting there saying, "There's nothing to all this." I warned him, as I warn everybody when I come to cast out demons. I know that you might make fun of some things but don't ever make fun of the real power of God. You are digging your own grave when you do that, besides you are getting mighty close to blaspheming the Holy Spirit when you make fun of the works of the Holy Ghost. I warned him, I warned the crowd, urging everyone to be reverent. But the man sat there and looked at me. I said, "All right, you'll take your responsibility, I won't. If you'll do as I say I'll take responsibility for you and nothing will happen to you." He took his own responsibility. Through the power of God, I cast the demons out of the man I was praying for. The dispossessed demons went through the audience seeking someone to enter. They struck this irreverent man a body blow and knocked him completely out of his chair onto the ground. The ushers found him writhing and twisting and biting his tongue and trying to scream out his misery. I told the ushers to bring him to me. They picked him up and carried him to me on the platform. It took me five minutes to get him delivered by the power of God. When he walked off that platform he was a different man. He will never make fun again. That has happened several times in our meetings and people have learned to fear God and know that God is alive in these last days. Now is the time to worship and reverence God, not to make fun of His holy power of deliverance.

I have seen demons control people, twisting and convulsing their bodies and tormenting their minds, making them scream out day and night. Oh, I hate the ugly power of the devil and his demon-world. God has put a love in my heart for demon-possessed people and I tell you now if you attend our meetings night after night you will see this power against demons. Over ten thousand demon-possessed people during the past few months have been healed! healed by the mighty power of Jesus of Nazareth in our meetings for Christ.

FAITH IN GOD ALONE DELIVERS

One night in Minneapolis, Minnesota, they brought a woman to our meeting from a psychopathic ward. They chained her to one of the tent poles behind the platform and called me back to pray for her. There was a minister who had a lot of zeal but not much knowledge who wanted to watch me as I brought God's deliverance to the demon-possessed. Before I could get to the woman chained to the pole he got ahead of me and ran over to her and said, "Oh Jesus, heal this person, heal this person." I knew he was treading on dangerous ground because it takes a lot more than zeal to get people healed. It takes *God's power!*

The woman began to curse and strike at him. I said, "My dear brother, step aside please." By that time he was scared half out of his wits. She had cursed him. I never heard such foul language. When demon-possessed people begin using blasphemous words it makes you shudder. I walked over to the woman without any fear because I was coming in the Name of Jesus. I felt his power coursing through my right hand already. I laid my hand on her head to pray. She looked up at me without a single curse word and I began to talk to the demons leering at me through her eyes that looked exactly like "snake eyes" and I called them out one by one in Jesus' Name. They began coming out. In a few seconds she was free. The wild look was gone from her face. I said to the minister near me, "There is a great difference in rushing into something like this and having God's faith in your heart to deal with demon-power! I allowed you to watch God's power working through me to let you see the *real* power of God over the power of demons."

KINDS OF DEMONS

There are many kinds of demons. The most powerful of all are the "unclean" demons. No unclean demon can enter a child of God because it cannot cross the bloodline of Christ. Neighbor, I am glad I am saved tonight! I am glad I am sanctified and filled with the Holy Spirit. When you are baptized with the Holy Ghost and fire there will be *no danger* of unclean spirits crossing the bloodline and possessing your life. I know that this wicked world sneers at the Holy Ghost and the *full gospel* people and I know the modern church tries to look down on us but we are the *safest*

people in the world. We are the safest people because we
have the Holy Spirit of God in us.

Now, demons work in three different ways. They work
either in the soul or the mind or the body. At rare times they
work in all—simultaneously. That is, a person can have unclean demons and be bound in soul, mind and body at the
same time. On the other hand, there are various kinds of
demons that work in the body of a person, even in the body
of a Christian. For instance, Jesus dealt with *deaf and dumb*
spirits. He called them that. So we know deaf and dumb
demons do take the hearing and speech of *some* people. Not
all deafness is caused by deaf and dumb spirits, it might be
caused by heredity; it might be caused by pneumonia or by
a fall or something like that, but there is a certain form of
deafness that will never respond to a hearing aid or anything
else except the healing power of Christ calling out the deaf
spirit. Then they can hear.

Jesus healed a woman whose body was *bound*. He said,
"Should not this woman be loosed whom satan hath bound,
lo these eighteen years," and He called out the *spirit of infirmity*. The spirit of infirmity. There was a demon in that
woman's body, a demon that had physically bound her.

Epilepsy has many causes. Sometimes it is organic in its
origin and sometimes it is caused by epileptic demons. I
have prayed for many people who were possessed with
epileptic demons, called in the Bible, "foul spirits." The old
Bible type of epilepsy—I say Bible type, I mean by that the
kind the Bible described in those days—that kind is caused
by epileptic spirits for Jesus said, "Thou foul spirits, come
out of him and enter no more into him." He said that to the
demons in the little child who was foaming at the mouth and
biting his tongue, writhing on the ground. You remember
the case. God's power works mightily in me against epileptic

demons. I cannot explain that except perhaps I have deeper compassion because of my sister's condition and because of great love for such people.

Then there are *lying demons*. There are sex demons, so that we have sex maniacs and sex perverts. A sex maniac is not made a sex maniac by an angel or by Jesus or by salvation or by the Holy Ghost. He is not made that way by common sense, he is not made that way by human birth. There is only one explanation for a sex maniac, he is possessed with unclean demons! How else would a grown man go out and rape a little six-year-old girl and chop her body in pieces? God did not do that and neither did common reason do that. There were real demons in him. I have dealt with many sex maniacs and sex perverts, both men and women and I know what it is to see them healed by God's power. I know there is only one hope and that hope is Jesus Christ. You cannot cure them by medicine, you cannot cure them by science or psychology, you cannot cure them by new resolutions but you can cure them by the power of the Son of God. Once the unclean demon is gone, the sex pervert is free and pure.

Demons are not the souls of lost people returned from hell and possessing other human beings. The Bible does not teach the transmigration of the human soul.

Demons are fallen angels who were once beautiful heavenly beings surrounding the throne of God. Led by Lucifer, ruler over the third part of the angels, they revolted against Almighty God and were cast out of heaven. Jesus said, "I beheld Satan as lightning fall from heaven."

Paul speaks of them as "principalities, powers, rulers of the darkness of this world" and of Satan (the fallen Lucifer) as "God of this world" and "prince of the powers of the air."

Lucifer has become the devil and the third part of the angels who followed him in rebellion and were cast out of heaven are demons who have headquarters between heaven and earth. The devil is "prince of the powers of the air." He walks about, up and down in the earth as a roaring lion, and the demons carry out his wicked orders. The power of these fearful personalities of evil is increased with each succeeding degree of man's disobedience against God. This is why there is so much demon-possession: mankind has gone astray from God, removing themselves from His protection by opening their hearts to sin. Unclean demons are most active where the presence of Christ is not felt.

The invisible demon-realm is located in the air, is located between us and God. To reach God, our faith must push its way through enemy territory. This is why our prayers are often beaten back in our faces. That is why sometimes our sermons are beaten back in our faces. That is why that sometimes the atmosphere is cold and chilled and we feel satanic pressure against us, for when we pray to God these demons are there to oppose us and to push our prayers back at us but God says, "Resist the devil and he shall flee from you." I believe that because I have practiced it and know it can be done. It is being done by people all over the world in Jesus' name.

There is only one place where an *unclean demon* cannot go and that is in the heart of a child of God. All other people are open to demon-power. I mean by that, they have no defense against unclean spirits. The only one defense is the name of Jesus Christ, the Son of God!

Russia's heart is shut up against God. (Christ's work is underground there.) Millions of demons are working in Russia with unbridled power because the presence of Christ is not there. That is what the people of America are up against. This is why we need more than bullets—we need God's healing power!

The spirit of antichrist is on the march. Everywhere preachers are saying, "Brother Roberts, isn't this the beginning of the last war? Are we facing the battle of Armageddon?" If we are, Christ is coming sooner than we think for Armageddon cannot come until Christ comes, and the antichrist cannot come until Jesus comes. If the antichrist is near, then thank God I'm ready for Jesus to come tonight! Without question we are in the drama of the end-time. There is an unfolding before us that is stranger than fiction, for all over this world we are locked in a titanic struggle against a kingdom of darkness controlled by Satan.

Demons are fallen angels. The demon who possesses a human being tonight has perhaps been in a thousand other persons in various generations and in various centuries from the time he was cast out of heaven. Jesus recognized demons and they knew him. The man who said his name was "Legion" who had a legion of demons (at least 2,000 of them) had never seen Jesus before and yet when He was a great way off, the demons, controlling him, cried out and said, "Jesus, we know who Thou art, Thou holy Son of God. Hast Thou come to torment us before our time?" They knew Him, they saw Him in heaven. Jesus knew them and commanded them to come out. They knew what power He had and they knew they were going to be tormented. Of course, all of the demons are awaiting the judgment of God. They are on the earth because of their rebellion against God and torment man because of his rebellion against God. The more sinful men get the more power demons have over them. The nearer we get to the end of time and men go farther from God, the more demons will work and have power over humankind. Men and women, if you ever intend to have

God's presence and to have Christ in your soul, do it now! And you who have backslidden, you of all people, are in most danger because you once knew God; now all the defense you ever had is gone and you are weakened even more than a person who never has been saved. All the faith-reflexes you had in use are now deflected. The most powerful cases of demon-possession I ever faced have been in backslidden people! If I were a backslider tonight, no one could keep me off my knees getting back with God!

HIGHER THAN CHRISTLESS MAN

Demons are higher than Christless man. The writer to the Hebrews wrote: "What is man that thou are mindful of him, or the son of man that thou visitest him, for thou hast made him a little lower than the angels. . . ." Also: ". . . But we see Jesus, who was made a little lower than the angels, for the suffering of death." Here is one of the strange things of God: the angels are a higher order of created beings, higher than natural man, so that man is a little lower than the angels. Now you see the power demons have over men.

God sent Jesus into the world to lift man to a level above angels. For Him to become our Saviour He had to become one of us. God could not send an angel to deliver us because a Saviour is One who goes through the same thing that you and I go through and then saves us! An angel is not a human being—a human being is not an angel. An angel cannot feel what I feel; I cannot feel what an angel feels, so God sent His own Son to be born as a human child, a baby, with human flesh. *"He was made a little lower than the angels."*

Let me explain this. Jesus was made bone of our bone, flesh of our flesh. Isaiah described Him as, ". . . a man of sorrows and acquainted with grief. He had no form or

comeliness that we would desire Him. He was bruised for
our iniquities, wounded for our transgressions and the
chastisement of our peace was upon Him, and by His stripes
we are healed. The Lord laid upon him the iniquity of us all.
We did esteem him stricken and smitten of God." The demons hounded Jesus and tried to kill him. They were there at
his birth in Bethlehem. They caused King Herod to be
jealous of the baby Jesus becoming King. Herod had hundreds of little boy babies killed and there was great lamen-
tation in Israel, of Ramah crying for her lost children.

Demons were there when Jesus preached in Nazareth, in
citing the people to hurl Jesus over the brow of the hill, but
he escaped out of their hands. Demons followed him and
opposed him. They were always afraid of him, and they
would scream, "Why hast thou come to torment us before
our time?" Yet Jesus used no weapon against them that is
not available to any child of God. "He was made a little
lower than the angels . . .", too. He was made as a man. Now
if you do not accept that, you do not accept the reality of
Jesus for He did not come into this world with the glory
he had before his birth. He laid aside His glory and was
born in the flesh. So they called him *Jesus.*

Jesus!

And they killed Him, and the wildest moment of joy and
jubilee Lucifer, or satan, ever had was the day of the crucifixion. It was a mob scene. Jesus said that the people did not
know what they did. Therefore he prayed, "Father, forgive
them." He knew that they were impelled by a mob spirit.
He knew the demons were there. Many Bible scholars believe that all the demons in the world were at Calvary the
day Christ died. They caused Judas to betray him with a
kiss after the "devil entered into him." They prevented
Pilate from releasing Jesus. With the speed of lightning the

demons hurled themselves across the universe into every nation, celebrating the victory of the death of Christ, and for three days Jesus was dead. A strange feeling came upon all the earth. Little did satan know that Jesus was now using the master-principle of deliverance. Little did he know that the master stroke of human liberation was about to be struck by the hand of the Son of God, for when they had him killed they simply released him from his human body. They did not kill *Christ*—they killed *Jesus! Jesus* was born in Bethlehem but *Christ* was alive when the morning stars sang together and before God laid the foundations of the earth!

Jesus lived among tortured, tormented humanity and was one of them, himself, "acquainted with grief." The human body was Jesus but that divine spirit was Christ! It was He who lay in the Father's bosom and said, "Let us make man." Death released Christ from the human body, that is all. In his resurrection he had, once again, the former glory He possessed before the foundations of the earth were laid.

Before the death and resurrection of Christ, when righteous people died they went into the upper part of a realm called *Hades*. When the wicked died they went in the lower part of the same place. Hades is a word for "hell." Before Christ's resurrection it was in two parts: upper and lower. Between them was an impassable gulf so that those in the upper part called *paradise* could not go into the part below, called *hell:* neither could those in hell ascend into the part above, called paradise. They were forever separated from each other. Now the spirit of Christ—released from his human body at death—went down into the upper part of Hades, called paradise. There "He preached to the spirits in prison." That is, He *proclaimed his victory on the Cross.* He told the righteous—Abraham, Isaac, Jacob, David and all other righteous people who had died looking forward to the coming of Christ the Messiah—how he had brought deliverance to humanity while he was on earth. He told them of his three-year ministry. Now he has come to set them free, to release them as "prisoners of hope" and transfer them from paradise in upper Hades *to heaven itself:* the immediate presence of God.

The captive souls of no-hope, those who had died without faith in the Messiah would remain in hell, the lower part of Hades, until the judgment day of God when they too would be transferred for judgment and for the sentence of eternal death. Hell remains unchanged.

The third morning dawned. Jesus rattled the gates of Hades and demanded the gate-keeper to open the gates. Demons hovered near to prevent his triumphal sweep to heaven leading "captivity captive."

Already the women were entering the Garden of Joseph. "Who will roll away the stone from his grave for us?" they whispered. Suddenly a brilliant light from heaven lighted up the tomb region. At that exact moment Jesus wrenched the gates of Hades off their hinges, grasped the keys of death, hell, and the grave, and sweeping up the souls of the *prisoners of hope* he swept up, up, up. Angels of God touched the stone over Jesus' tomb and rolled it away. The Son of God rose from the rock slab, walked out of the tomb and pausing a moment, he shouted,

> *"Because I live, ye shall live also!"*

Soon he vanished. The women rushed up and found the stone rolled away. The angel said, "Ye seek Jesus. He is not here, He is risen. Behold the place where the Lord lay!" Mary did not understand. She began to hunt the Lord and when she saw a stranger she supposed Him to be the gardener. She said, "Sir, where have you borne Him?"

He said, "Mary!"

"Master!"

She reached out to touch Him. He said, "Touch me not for I am not yet ascended to your God and My God—My Father and your Father." Then gathering up *captivity* in His hands He ascended far above all principalities; above kingdoms; above the devil's headquarters; above the spirit realm of demon spirits; far above every name, every kingdom; above every principality. Across heaven rang the cry:

"Lift up your heads, O ye gates—ye everlasting doors; and the King of glory shall come in
Who is this King of glory?
The Lord of Hosts, he is the King of Glory."

The Son of God passed through the gates of glory, down the streets of gold and laid the souls of the ransomed at the feet of the Father. He sat down on the Father's right hand, opened up the vaults of heaven, brought forth the nine gifts of the spirit and gave gifts unto men. Now John says, "Greater is He that is in you, than he that is in the world." With the resurrection of Christ the gifts of God were poured out. Now when a person receives Christ as his Saviour who has ascended far above all angels and principalities and kingdoms, he is given status *above* the angels with *power over demon spirits!* Jesus says, "These signs shall follow them who believe, in my name they shall cast out demons."

Believers in Christ are higher than angels. God gives them power against demon spirits. The only hope of the world is in the followers of Jesus Christ. People, we have a job to do for God! Aren't you glad you have been saved? Aren't you glad you are a Christian? Aren't you glad you are alive to-night? Aren't you glad that Jesus Christ is coming soon and God is dealing with us and giving us power to deal with

demon spirits, and to cast them out and to do a great work
for Jesus Christ in these last days? If you are, say, "Amen!"

In Ada, Oklahoma, where I was raised as a boy—we took
our big tent back there two years ago September last for a
meeting within a block and a half of where I was healed of
T.B. In that meeting, my oldest brother, Elmer, brought a
man for healing. Some of the children of this man had
asked Elmer to bring him. The man had lost his mind. He
was a prominent church man. He loved Jesus but through
the death of his wife he had become depressed and even-
tually had gone insane. Powerful mental demons robbed
him of his mind. Now that man, had he died in that condition would have gone to heaven because he was a saved
man. People who become insane without being saved (if
they are old enough to know what being saved is) will lose
their souls if they die in that condition. It depends a lot
upon the condition one is in when certain things happen to you. This man was a good man. My oldest brother
told me about him. He said, "Oral, he's 72 years old and
he's a good man. He's been in the insane asylum and his
children asked me to come to you, since I was your brother,
and they said they can't keep him out after 6:00 o'clock."
They wanted to know if I would pray for him privately
and I told them, "No, I don't pray for people privately. God
didn't call me to a private ministry." I said, "If you cannot
get his release after 6:00 o'clock, you'll have to take him
back." Not because I was without compassion; I simply do
as God directs me. This may sound strange to others but
it is perfectly clear to me. They got the man released a
little longer and brought him to the tent where he was
given a seat behind the platform and left there until after
I preached. They wanted me to stop preaching and pray for
him. People are strange, they think only of themselves, they

do not often think of anybody else. The sermon that night won over 200 souls to Christ. I felt the saving of 200 souls was worth more than a miracle of healing. What did one more hour matter when souls might be saved? People are selfish! That is one reason why some people will never be healed; they are too selfish to be healed. You must prefer others before you and be meek and humble in the presence of God. The greatest thing in the world is the preaching of the gospel. I believe "Faith cometh by hearing and hearing by the word of God." If you do not want the word of God, you will not get healed anyway. I must do more than pray to get people healed. Listen, folks, if you don't let me preach the word of God to strengthen your faith in God, I cannot help you. I have no power outside this Bible, the holy word of God. When you go to church, let your preacher preach. We have some folks who don't want him to preach. We have some folks who will do anything to get him to stop preaching. I have always wondered about folks who give so-called special messages while God's word is going forth. Seems to me that God's message should come first before anything comes.

Well, let us get back to this man. When I got through preaching and leading over 200 souls to Christ I went back and rested three or four minutes; then I went to minister to the man who was insane. My oldest brother directed me to him. His children were standing around the old man and I stood before him and put my hand on his head and started to pray. But I could not feel God's power to deliver him. Finally the Lord impressed me to pull him close to me and put his arms around me and put my arms around him. When I did this I got all broken up and I felt God's healing power go out of my hand and God healed him. I said to him, "What's your name?" He told me what his name was,

and I said, "Who is this?" He called the name of his child
I was pointing to. God healed him that night and made him
perfectly whole, restoring his mind. They got his release
from the insane asylum in a matter of days and he came back
to his church perfectly whole by God's power.

GREATEST MIRACLE

The greatest miracle I have ever seen in our meetings
occurred just a few months ago. Here is how it happened.
This is going to sound strange to you, but don't judge it
until I get through. A woman missionary was possessed
with demon spirits! It was a peculiar case. She was a young
woman of some thirty-five years of age. She was one of the
finest women that the Mission Board had ever sent forth.
But they sent her alone to the wilds of darkest Africa. She
ministered in the remote forests of Africa where witchcraft
and voodooism abounded. She worked for years and wore
her strength down. Demons controlled the people, soul and
body. *Wherever the gospel of Christ has not been preached,
demons rule the people.* She worked alone—for too long.
When she got discouraged she had nobody to turn to, when
she got weak in body she had nobody to pray for her. This
is why we ought to pray for our missionaries and hold them
up in prayer. They represent God, they are *our* missionaries.
We ought to pray for them.

Finally she broke in health. Without help she could not
withstand the constant pressure of the demon-world against
her. She had a nervous breakdown and the demons pounced
upon her and took her mind. They brought her home
wrecked in mind and put her in a psychopathic ward. Her
pastor brought her to our healing campaign.

"Brother Roberts," he said, "we have a missionary, member of my church, who is in a psychopathic ward of the insane asylum; she's in a padded cell. She's very violent and is very destructive and will kill herself if they don't guard her."

He went on to say that she loved God, but she had broken down and in that weakened condition these powers had seized her mind.

He said, "Brother Roberts, I have gone to the hospital many times and prayed for her but I have not yet reached her. Will you permit us to bring her to this meeting for healing?"

Well now, that's a serious thing. We seldom receive violent cases because it is not always safe to bring them in a crowd. I said, "All right, you can bring her. Put her behind the platform and have somebody to guard her while I preach. When I get through preaching, I'll come back behind the platform and pray for her." He did. They guarded her while I preached.

After preaching and leading the unsaved to Christ, I went back behind the platform. I had a strange feeling as I started to pray for her. I said to her pastor, "Put her in the healing line." She seemed perfectly quiet that night, perfectly all right. I am always happy to have folks in the public line if there is any way to get them there. It is better, of course, to pray for emergency cases behind the platform, or in a room separated from the curious eyes of people where they can relax and I can take time with them. We always do that to protect the people.

He got her by the arm and spoke soothingly to her and brought her around the platform to our left and put her in the healing line. I was sitting in a chair where the people passed by me on the lower platform. Dr. Sproull was in his customary place taking the cards from the people as they passed by. I saw the woman coming. I felt those powerful spirits. I always feel them. Once in a while I make a mistake, I am not perfect, but I felt them that night. When she got up in front of me, Dr. Sproull took the card. Her pastor had gone up on the platform and sat down. She stood in front of me. As usual I had the people to bow their heads, and I warned them not to raise their heads while those demons were coming out. I reached over to put my hand on her head when she leered at me. She said, "I'm going to hurt you! I'm going to kill you!"

I said, "No, you're not going to hurt me." I had dealt with cases like that before, but never one that did like she did a moment later.

I said, "No, you're not going to hurt me," and I started to put my right hand on her head. When I did she reached up and grabbed my arm and jerked me off that platform like I was a child. I started to her a second time when she took hold of my coat and ripped it in front, and jerked the buttons off. She was a raving maniac. I had never dealt with a person who had the strength she had. Those powerful demons had almost made her into a super-human. When I started toward her, she simply shoved me back. Now I am a strong man, but she shoved me with ease. I saw Dr. Sproull out of the corner of my eye start toward me; my brother Vaden started in a run toward me. Nobody has ever come to help me because so far I have never needed help, but Vaden started running toward me that night.

I knew if I could ever get my right hand on her head I would be all right, but I couldn't get to her. Every time I would start her, she would shove me back. She was actually trying to kill me! I heard a gasp of astonishment from the great audience; they knew something was happening. The demon power was so powerful I could scarcely breathe, and she was saying all kinds of terrible things. But it wasn't she who was talking. The demons had control of her tongue.

I watched her. I watched how she maneuvered her hands and finally I caught her off guard a moment and took my hands and pulled her arms apart and shoved my right hand on her head. The moment I did, the battle was almost over. When I got my hand on her head, the power of God was like *liquid fire* shooting through my right hand. I detected the presence of 14 demon spirits that controlled her mind and were torturing her like that. I began to call the demons out. I spoke to the crowd, "Don't anybody raise your head for Jesus' sake!" I had my hand on her head and I began to say, "Thou foul mental demons, I adjure thee in Jesus' name, come out!" Like you turn the pages of a book I felt them, one by one, as they began to leave and I cried out, "There they go, there they go!" A great spirit of joy started in the pit of my stomach and kept coming up within me. I felt them go. When the last one was gone, there was no pressure against my hand. Great joy filled my soul. I shouted, "They're out of her," and when I did she looked up and the light of God was in her face, and she said, "I'm free! I'm free! I'm free!" Oh brother, the people raised their heads and put their hands up and shouted for joy. Her pastor was sitting over to my left and he said, "Brother Roberts, Brother Roberts! Did you call my name?"

I said, "No."

He said, "Did Brother Sproull?"

I said, "No, Brother Sproull didn't."

He said, "Somebody called my name."

I said, "It was God who called your name."

God called his name that night, sitting there on the platform, and he said God told him certain things. I don't doubt it. I know that "Where sin doth abound, grace doth much more abound" and I mean by that statement where demons abound, God's angels are there to deliver. Remember, only one-third of the angels fell—two-thirds did not! *We happen to be on the winning side!* For every *one* demon, there are *two* angels—for every ten demons there are twenty angels there to help us and to deliver us. Glory to the name of Jesus!

LEGION IS HEALED

But that miracle does not compare with another miracle. Go back with me tonight 2000 years, take a trip with me across the sea of Galilee, please. Jesus is with his twelve disciples, He is going to Gadara, the land of the demon-possessed. There was a region across the sea of Galilee, called Gadara, where the civil and religious authorities huddled their insane and demon-possessed people together. They lived in the "valley of the tombs." Their leader's name was Legion. When they chained him, he would break the chains in two. Jesus went to deliver him. It was late in the evening, and here's what happened: They anchored the little boat on the Gadarene side, climbed out of the boat and walked ashore. All of a sudden they were startled by a wild cry as of something untamed, whether of man or beast, it was hard to tell.

There appeared on the brow of the hill, a wild man, completely naked, who was screaming at the top of his voice. The disciples jerked their swords out and stood tense, expecting an attack. Someone said Judas Iscariot clutched his moneybag and slunk away and got back in the boat and covered himself up with one of the cloaks. Jesus did not so much as shift His position. This wild man drew himself up to his full height, plunged forward and raced down the hill, like a wild animal and began circling Jesus and screaming, "Jesus, Thou Son of God, hast Thou come to torment us before our time?"

Jesus raised his voice and said, "What is thy name?"

He said, "Legion, for we are many."

Jesus said, "I command thee, thou unclean spirits, come out of him."

The man twisted, jerked, leaped in the air and ran hurriedly toward Jesus. He raised up his hands to strike Him, Jesus lifted His right hand and said,

"Peace!"

He stopped. His huge hands fell to his sides. The fires of insanity died out in his eyes; his muscles relaxed, the tension went out of his body. He looked around in obvious amazement. His eyes fell on Jesus. He said, "Master! Master!" When he saw Jesus he looked at himself and realized he was naked. He said, "Master! I am naked."

Jesus said, "Get some clothes for him." They put clothes on him. He stood there in his right mind before Jesus and his disciples. When they got back in the boat and he saw they were about to leave, he said, "Wait a minute! Master! Wait a minute!"

They waited, and he climbed on board, walked up to Jesus, fell down before Him and said, "Master! You have healed me! You have brought peace to me! You have called the demons out of me! Master, will you let me go with You wherever You go?"

Jesus said, "Young man, go home and tell the people what the Lord has done for you." He saluted the disciples, shook the hand of the Lord, got off the boat, ran up the hill and through the valley of the tombs, shouting at the top of his voice that Jesus had healed him.

When he got near the city of Gadara, the gatekeepers

heard him. They said, "Legion, Legion—Legion is coming!"
They cried, "Bolt the doors!" They were closing the gate of
the city when they heard Legion say, "Men of Gadara! Do
not be afraid, Jesus of Nazareth has healed me!"

They said, "What's this? Is this some trick?"

Many times they had tried to bind him only to have him
snap the chains and brutally attack them, so they stood back.

Legion walked up and said, "Men, see, I have on clothes!
Look at my eyes, look at my face. I'm all right. *Jesus* made
me whole." But news had already preceded him and men
had left their work and children had left their play. People
of Gadara locked their doors because this wild man had
torn up their town the last time he was there. He hurried
down the streets toward his home. Down at the end of the
lane in the little vine-covered shack was his family. His wife
bore on her body the marks and bruises made by his cruel
hands and she was afraid. Somebody said, "Oh, Mrs. Legion!
Mrs. Legion! Legion is coming!"

She said, "Children—come quick." They came to her and
she got them in the house. She heard Legion coming. She
said, "What's he saying? What's that he's saying?" She heard
his loud voice speaking to his neighbors, "Neighbors, don't
be afraid of me! I am all right!"

She said, "Children, something has happened to your
father." Then she heard him sing and she said, "I *know*
something's happened to him," and she stood there trembling.

He turned the corner and she said, "He's got clothes on!
He's got clothes on!" He came to the gate and stood there
smiling and praising God. She said, "Legion! What's happened to you?"

He opened the gate and said, "Honey, don't be afraid!
See, I have on clothes. I'm all right," and he came up and

took her hands in his and she said, "But Legion, Legion, are you sure you're all right?" He said, "Yes, I'm all right, honey." She said, "What's happened to you?" He said,

"I met the Master and he mastered me."

Oh, men and women of these last days, this is deliverance! This is Bible Deliverance! Do you believe it tonight?

Every head bowed, please.